ISBN: 978-1-6413-6684-7

First Edition: Dhūl Hijjah 1438 A.H. /September 2017 C.E.

Cover Design: Usul Designs

Translation by Umm ʿĀʾishah Rumaysah Bond
Revision & Editing by ʿAbdullāh Omrān

Typesetting & formatting by
Abū Sulaymān Muḥammad ʿAbdul-ʿAẓīm Ibn Joshua Baker

Printing: Ohio Printing

Subject: Usul Deen/ Tawhīd/ ʿAqīdah

Website : www.maktabatul-irshad.com

00316 41 58 59 64

مكتبة الإرشاد
Maktabatul-Irshad
PUBLICATIONS

فهرس

Table of Contents

ARABIC TEXT

بسم الله الرحمن الرحيم

اِعْلَمْ - رَحِمَكَ اللهُ - أَنَّهُ يَجِبُ عَلَيْنَا تَعَلُّمُ أَرْبَعِ مَسَائِلَ ,اَلْأُولَى: اَلْعِلْمُ وَ هُوَ مَعْرِفَةُ اللهِ, وَمَعْرِفَةُ نَبِيِّهِ, وَمَعْرِفَةُ دِينِ الْإِسْلَامِ بِالْأَدِلَّةِ. اَلثَّانِيَةُ : اَلْعَمَلُ بِهِ اَلثَّالِثَةُ : الدَّعْوَةُ إِلَيْهِ. اَلرَّابِعَةُ: اَلصَّبْرُ عَلَى الْأَذَى فِيهِ. وَالدَّلِيلُ قَوْلُهُ تَعَالَى : ﴿وَٱلْعَصْرِ ① إِنَّ ٱلْإِنسَـٰنَ لَفِى خُسْرٍ ② إِلَّا ٱلَّذِينَ ءَامَنُوا۟ وَعَمِلُوا۟ ٱلصَّـٰلِحَـٰتِ وَتَوَاصَوْا۟ بِٱلْحَقِّ وَتَوَاصَوْا۟ بِٱلصَّبْرِ ③﴾ [العصر:١ – ٣]. قَالَ الشَّافِعِي - رَحِمَهُ اللهُ - : لَوْ مَا أَنْزَلَ اللهُ حُجَّةً عَلَى خَلْقِهِ إِلَّا هَذِهِ السُّورَةَ لَكَفَتْهُمْ وَ قَالَ الْبُخَارِي – رَحِمَهُ اللهُ تَعَالَى - : بَابُ الْعِلْمِ قَبْلَ الْقَوْلِ وَ الْعَمَلِ. وَالدَّلِيلُ : ﴿فَٱعْلَمْ أَنَّهُۥ لَآ إِلَـٰهَ إِلَّا ٱللَّهُ وَٱسْتَغْفِرْ لِذَنۢبِكَ﴾ [محمد: ١٩] . فَبَدَأَ بِالْعِلْمِ قَبْلَ الْقَوْلِ وَ الْعَمَلِ. اِعْلَمْ - رَحِمَكَ اللهُ – أَنَّهُ يَجِبُ عَلَى كُلِّ مُسْلِمٍ وَ مُسْلِمَةٍ تَعَلُّمُ ثَلَاثِ هَذِهِ

الْمَسَائِلِ وَ الْعَمَلُ بِهِنَّ. اَلْأُولَى: أَنَّ اللهَ خَلَقَنَا وَ رَزَقَنَا, وَلَمْ يَتْرُكْنَا هَمَلاً. بَلْ أَرْسَلَ إِلَيْنَا رَسُولاً. فَمَنْ أَطَاعَهُ دَخَلَ الْجَنَّةَ, وَ مَنْ عَصَاهُ دَخَلَ النَّارَ. وَالدَّلِيلُ قَوْلُهُ تَعَالَى: ﴿إِنَّآ أَرْسَلْنَآ إِلَيْكُمْ رَسُولًا شَٰهِدًا عَلَيْكُمْ كَمَآ أَرْسَلْنَآ إِلَىٰ فِرْعَوْنَ رَسُولًا ﴿١٥﴾ فَعَصَىٰ فِرْعَوْنُ ٱلرَّسُولَ فَأَخَذْنَٰهُ أَخْذًا وَبِيلًا ﴿١٦﴾﴾ [المزمل: ١٥ – ١٦]. اَلثَّانِيَةُ: أَنَّ اللهَ لَا يَرْضَى أَنْ يُشْرَكَ مَعَهُ أَحَدٌ فِي عِبَادَتِهِ, لَا مَلَكٌ مُقَرَّبٌ وَ لَا نَبِيٌّ مُرْسَلٌ. وَ الدَّلِيلُ قَوْلُهُ تَعَالَى: ﴿وَأَنَّ ٱلْمَسَٰجِدَ لِلَّهِ فَلَا تَدْعُوا۟ مَعَ ٱللَّهِ أَحَدًا ﴿١٨﴾﴾ [الجن: ١٨]. اَلثَّالِثَةُ: أَنَّ مَنْ أَطَاعَ الرَّسُولَ, وَ وَحَّدَ اللهَ, لَا يَجُوزُ لَهُ مُوَالَاةُ مَنْ حَادَّ اللهَ وَ رَسُولَهُ وَ لَوْ كَانَ أَقْرَبَ قَرِيبٍ وَالدَّلِيلُ قَوْلُهُ تَعَالَى: ﴿لَّا تَجِدُ قَوْمًا يُؤْمِنُونَ بِٱللَّهِ وَٱلْيَوْمِ ٱلْءَاخِرِ يُوَآدُّونَ مَنْ حَآدَّ ٱللَّهَ وَرَسُولَهُۥ وَلَوْ كَانُوٓا۟ ءَابَآءَهُمْ أَوْ أَبْنَآءَهُمْ أَوْ إِخْوَٰنَهُمْ أَوْ عَشِيرَتَهُمْ ۚ أُو۟لَٰٓئِكَ كَتَبَ فِى قُلُوبِهِمُ ٱلْإِيمَٰنَ وَأَيَّدَهُم بِرُوحٍ مِّنْهُ ۖ وَيُدْخِلُهُمْ جَنَّٰتٍ تَجْرِى مِن تَحْتِهَا ٱلْأَنْهَٰرُ خَٰلِدِينَ فِيهَا ۚ رَضِىَ ٱللَّهُ عَنْهُمْ وَرَضُوا۟ عَنْهُ ۚ أُو۟لَٰٓئِكَ حِزْبُ ٱللَّهِ ۚ أَلَآ إِنَّ حِزْبَ ٱللَّهِ هُمُ ٱلْمُفْلِحُونَ ﴿٢٢﴾﴾ [المجادلة: ٢٢]. اِعْلَمْ أَرْشَدَكَ اللهُ لِطَاعَتِهِ, أَنَّ

الْـحَـنِـيـفِـيَّـةَ مِـلَّـةَ إِبْـرَاهِـيـمَ أَنْ تَـعْـبُـدَ اللهَ مُـخْـلِـصًـا لَـهُ الـدِّيـنَ. وَ بِـذَلِـكَ أَمَـرَ اللهُ جَـمِـيـعَ الـنَّـاسِ, وَ خَـلَـقَـهُـمْ لَـهَـا كَـمَـا قَـالَ تَـعَـالَـى : ﴿ وَمَا خَلَقْتُ ٱلْجِنَّ وَٱلْإِنسَ إِلَّا لِيَعْبُدُونِ ﴿٥٦﴾ ﴾ [الذاريات: ٥٦]. وَ مَـعْـنَـى (يَـعْـبُـدُونِ) : يُـوَحِّـدُونِ .وَ أَعْـظَـمُ مَـا أَمَـرَ اللهُ بِـهِ الـتَّـوْحِـيـدُ, وَ هُـوَ إِفْـرَادُ اللهِ بِـالْـعِـبَـادَةِ, وَ أَعْـظَـمُ مَـا نَـهَـى عَـنْـهُ الـشِّـرْكُ, وَ هُـوَ دَعْـوَةُ غَـيْـرِهِ مَـعَـهُ وَ الـدَّلِـيـلُ قَـوْلُـهُ تَـعَـالَـى : ﴿ ۞ وَٱعْبُدُوا۟ ٱللَّهَ وَلَا تُشْرِكُوا۟ بِهِۦ شَيْـًٔا ﴾ [النساء: ٣٦]. فَـإِذَا قِـيـلَ لَـكَ : مَـا الْأُصُـولُ الـثَّـلَاثَـةُ الَّـتِـي يَـجِـبُ عَـلَـى الْإِنْـسَـانِ مَـعْـرِفَـتُـهَـا ؟ فَـقُـلْ : مَـعْـرِفَـةُ الْـعَـبْـدِ رَبَّـهُ, وَ دِيـنَـهُ, وَ نَـبِـيَّـهُ مُـحَـمَّـدًا – صَـلَّـى اللهُ عَـلَـيْـهِ وَ سَـلَّـمَ. فَـإِذَا قِـيـلَ لَـكَ : مَـنْ رَبُّـكَ ؟ فَـقُـلْ : رَبِّـي اللهُ الَّـذِي رَبَّـانِـي وَ رَبَّـى جَـمِـيـعَ الْـعَـالَـمِـيـنَ بِـنِـعَـمِـهِ .وَ هُـوَ مَـعْـبُـودِي لَـيْـسَ لِـي مَـعْـبُـودٌ سِـوَاهُ . وَالـدَّلِـيـلُ قَـوْلُـهُ تَـعَـالَـى : ﴿ ٱلْحَمْدُ لِلَّهِ رَبِّ ٱلْعَٰلَمِينَ ﴿٢﴾ ﴾ [الفاتحة: ٢] وَ كُـلُّ مَـا سِـوَى اللهِ عَـالَـمٌ وَ أَنَـا وَاحِـدٌ مِـنْ ذَلِـكَ الْـعَـالَـمِ . فَـإِذَا قِـيـلَ لَـكَ : بِـمَـا عَـرَفْـتَ رَبَّـكَ ؟ فَـقُـلْ : بِـآيَـاتِـهِ وَ مَـخْـلُـوقَـاتِـهِ. وَ مِـنْ آيَـاتِـهِ الـلَّـيْـلُ وَ الـنَّـهَـارُ وَ الـشَّـمْـسُ وَ

الْقَمَرُ. وَمِنْ مَخْلُوقَاتِهِ: السَّمَوَاتُ السَّبْعُ, وَ الْأَرَضُونَ السَّبْعُ وَ مَا فِيهِنَّ, وَ مَا بَيْنَهُمَا, وَ الدَّلِيلُ قَوْلُهُ تَعَالَى: ﴿ وَمِنْ ءَايَـٰتِهِ ٱلَّيْلُ وَٱلنَّهَارُ وَٱلشَّمْسُ وَٱلْقَمَرُ ۚ لَا تَسْجُدُوا۟ لِلشَّمْسِ وَلَا لِلْقَمَرِ وَٱسْجُدُوا۟ لِلَّهِ ٱلَّذِى خَلَقَهُنَّ إِن كُنتُمْ إِيَّاهُ تَعْبُدُونَ ﴿٣٧﴾ ﴾ [فصلت: ٣٧] وَ الدَّلِيلُ قَوْلُهُ تَعَالَى: ﴿ إِنَّ رَبَّكُمُ ٱللَّهُ ٱلَّذِى خَلَقَ ٱلسَّمَـٰوَٰتِ وَٱلْأَرْضَ فِى سِتَّةِ أَيَّامٍ ثُمَّ ٱسْتَوَىٰ عَلَى ٱلْعَرْشِ يُغْشِى ٱلَّيْلَ ٱلنَّهَارَ يَطْلُبُهُۥ حَثِيثًا وَٱلشَّمْسَ وَٱلْقَمَرَ وَٱلنُّجُومَ مُسَخَّرَٰتٍۭ بِأَمْرِهِۦٓ ۗ أَلَا لَهُ ٱلْخَلْقُ وَٱلْأَمْرُ ۗ تَبَارَكَ ٱللَّهُ رَبُّ ٱلْعَـٰلَمِينَ ﴿٥٤﴾ ﴾ [الأعراف: ٥٤] وَ الرَّبُّ هُوَ الْمَعْبُودُ, وَ الدَّلِيلُ قَوْلُهُ: ﴿ يَـٰٓأَيُّهَا ٱلنَّاسُ ٱعْبُدُوا۟ رَبَّكُمُ ٱلَّذِى خَلَقَكُمْ وَٱلَّذِينَ مِن قَبْلِكُمْ لَعَلَّكُمْ تَتَّقُونَ ﴿٢١﴾ ٱلَّذِى جَعَلَ لَكُمُ ٱلْأَرْضَ فِرَٰشًا وَٱلسَّمَآءَ بِنَآءً وَأَنزَلَ مِنَ ٱلسَّمَآءِ مَآءً فَأَخْرَجَ بِهِۦ مِنَ ٱلثَّمَرَٰتِ رِزْقًا لَّكُمْ ۖ فَلَا تَجْعَلُوا۟ لِلَّهِ أَندَادًا وَأَنتُمْ تَعْلَمُونَ ﴿٢٢﴾ ﴾ [البقرة: ٢١ – ٢٢]. قَالَ ابْنُ كَثِيرٍ: الْخَالِقُ لِهَذِهِ الْأَشْيَاءِ هُوَ الْمُسْتَحِقُّ لِلْعِبَادَةِ. وَأَنْوَاعُ الْعِبَادَةِ الَّتِي أَمَرَ اللهُ بِهَا مِثْلَ الْإِسْلَامِ وَ الْإِيمَانِ وَ الْإِحْسَانِ, وَ مِنْهُ الدُّعَاءُ, وَ الْخَوْفُ, وَ الرَّجَاءُ, وَ التَّوَكُّلُ, وَ الرَّغْبَةُ, وَ الرَّهْبَةُ, وَ

الْخُشُوعُ, وَالْخَشْيَةُ, وَالْإِنَابَةُ, وَالْإِسْتِعَانَةُ, وَالْإِسْتِعَاذَةُ
, وَالْإِسْتِغَاثَةُ, وَالذَّبْحُ, وَالنَّذْرُ, وَ غَيْرُ ذَلِكَ مِنْ أَنْوَاعِ
الْعِبَادَةِ الَّتِي أَمَرَ اللهُ بِهَا, كُلُّهَا للهِ تَعَالَى. وَ الدَّلِيلُ
قَوْلُهُ تَعَالَى: ﴿وَأَنَّ ٱلْمَسَٰجِدَ لِلَّهِ فَلَا تَدْعُوا۟ مَعَ ٱللَّهِ أَحَدًا ١٨﴾ [الجن: ١٨
]. فَمَنْ صَرَفَ مِنْهَا شَيْئًا لِغَيْرِ اللهِ, فَهُوَ مُشْرِكٌ كَافِرٌ
وَ الدَّلِيلُ قَوْلُهُ تَعَالَى: ﴿وَمَن يَدْعُ مَعَ ٱللَّهِ إِلَٰهًا ءَاخَرَ لَا بُرْهَٰنَ لَهُۥ
بِهِۦ فَإِنَّمَا حِسَابُهُۥ عِندَ رَبِّهِۦٓ ۚ إِنَّهُۥ لَا يُفْلِحُ ٱلْكَٰفِرُونَ ١١٧﴾ [المؤمنون: ١١٧]. وَ
فِي الْحَدِيثِ: ((الدُّعَاءُ مُخُّ الْعِبَادَةِ)). وَ الدَّلِيلُ: قَوْلُهُ
تَعَالَى: ﴿وَقَالَ رَبُّكُمُ ٱدْعُونِىٓ أَسْتَجِبْ لَكُمْ ۚ إِنَّ ٱلَّذِينَ يَسْتَكْبِرُونَ عَنْ
عِبَادَتِى سَيَدْخُلُونَ جَهَنَّمَ دَاخِرِينَ ٦٠﴾ [غافر: ٦٠]. وَ دَلِيلُ الْخَوْفِ
قَوْلُهُ تَعَالَى: ﴿فَلَا تَخَافُوهُمْ وَخَافُونِ إِن كُنتُم مُّؤْمِنِينَ ١٧٥﴾ [آل عمران:
١٧٥]. وَ دَلِيلُ الرَّجَاءِ قَوْلُهُ تَعَالَى: ﴿فَمَن كَانَ يَرْجُوا۟ لِقَآءَ رَبِّهِۦ فَلْيَعْمَلْ
عَمَلًا صَٰلِحًا وَلَا يُشْرِكْ بِعِبَادَةِ رَبِّهِۦٓ أَحَدًا ١١٠﴾ [الكهف: ١١٠]. وَ دَلِيلُ
التَّوَكُّلِ قَوْلُهُ تَعَالَى: ﴿وَعَلَى ٱللَّهِ فَتَوَكَّلُوٓا۟ إِن كُنتُم مُّؤْمِنِينَ ٢٣﴾
[المائدة: ٢٣]. وَ قَوْلُهُ تَعَالَى: ﴿وَمَن يَتَوَكَّلْ عَلَى ٱللَّهِ فَهُوَ حَسْبُهُۥٓ ۚ﴾

[الطلاق: ٣]. وَ دَلِيلُ الرَّغْبَةِ وَ الرَّهْبَةِ وَ الْخُشُوعِ قَوْلُهُ تَعَالَى : ﴿إِنَّهُمْ كَانُوا۟ يُسَٰرِعُونَ فِى ٱلْخَيْرَٰتِ وَيَدْعُونَنَا رَغَبًا وَرَهَبًا ۖ وَكَانُوا۟ لَنَا خَٰشِعِينَ ﴿٩٠﴾﴾ [الأنبياء: ٩٠]. وَ دَلِيلُ الْخَشْيَةِ قَوْلُهُ تَعَالَى : ﴿فَلَا تَخْشَوْهُمْ وَٱخْشَوْنِى﴾ [البقرة: ١٥٠] . وَ دَلِيلُ الْإِنَابَةِ قَوْلُهُ : ﴿وَأَنِيبُوٓا۟ إِلَىٰ رَبِّكُمْ وَأَسْلِمُوا۟ لَهُۥ﴾ [الزمر: ٥٤]. وَ دَلِيلُ الْإِسْتِعَانَةِ قَوْلُهُ تَعَالَى : ﴿إِيَّاكَ نَعْبُدُ وَإِيَّاكَ نَسْتَعِينُ ﴿٥﴾﴾ [الفاتحة: ٥] . وَ فِي الْحَدِيثِ : ((إِذَا اسْتَعَنْتَ فَاسْتَعِنْ بِاللهِ)) وَ دَلِيلُ الْإِسْتِعَاذَةِ قَوْلُهُ تَعَالَى : ﴿قُلْ أَعُوذُ بِرَبِّ ٱلْفَلَقِ ﴿١﴾﴾ [الفلق: ١]. وَ قَوْلُهُ تَعَالَى : ﴿قُلْ أَعُوذُ بِرَبِّ ٱلنَّاسِ ﴿١﴾﴾ [الناس: ١]. وَ دَلِيلُ الْإِسْتِغَاثَةِ قَوْلُهُ تَعَالَى : ﴿إِذْ تَسْتَغِيثُونَ رَبَّكُمْ فَٱسْتَجَابَ لَكُمْ﴾ [الأنفال: ٩]. وَ دَلِيلُ الذَّبْحِ قَوْلُهُ تَعَالَى : ﴿قُلْ إِنَّ صَلَاتِى وَنُسُكِى وَمَحْيَاىَ وَمَمَاتِى لِلَّهِ رَبِّ ٱلْعَٰلَمِينَ ﴿١٦٢﴾ لَا شَرِيكَ لَهُۥ ۖ وَبِذَٰلِكَ أُمِرْتُ وَأَنَا۠ أَوَّلُ ٱلْمُسْلِمِينَ ﴿١٦٣﴾﴾ [الأنعام: ١٦٢ – ١٦٣]. وَ مِنَ السُّنَّةِ : ((لَعَنَ اللهُ

مَـنْ ذَبَـحَ لِـغَـيْـرِ اللهِ)) وَ دَلِـيـلُ الـنَّـذرِ قَـوْلُـهُ تَـعَـالَـى : ﴿ يُوفُونَ بِالنَّذْرِ وَيَخَافُونَ يَوْمًا كَانَ شَرُّهُۥ مُسْتَطِيرًا ﴿٧﴾ ﴾ [الإنسان: ٧].

اَلْأَصْلُ الثَّانِي : مَـعْـرِفَـةُ دِيـنِ الْإِسْـلَامِ بِـالْأَدِلَّـةِ . هُـوَ الِاسْـتِـسْـلَامُ لِله بِـالـتَّـوْحِـيـدِ , وَالِانْـقِـيَـادُ لَـهُ بِـالـطَّـاعَـةِ . وَ الْـبَـرَاءَةُ مِـنَ الـشِّـرْكِ وَ أَهْـلِـهِ . وَهُـوَ ثَـلَاثُ مَـرَاتِـبَ : الْإِسْلَامُ , وَ الْإِيـمَـانُ , وَ الْإِحْـسَـانُ , وَ كُـلُّ مَـرْتَـبَـةٍ لَـهَـا أَرْكَـانٌ . فَـأَرْكَـانُ الْإِسْـلَامِ خَـمْـسَـةٌ : شَـهَـادَةُ أَنْ لَا إِلَـهَ إِلَّا اللهُ , وَ أَنَّ مُـحَـمَّـدًا رَسُـولُ اللهِ (صَـلَّـى اللهُ عَـلَـيْـهِ وَ سَـلَّـمَ) , وَ إِقَـامُ الـصَّـلَاةِ وَ إِيْـتَـاءُ الـزَّكَـاةِ , وَ صَـوْمُ رَمَـضَـانَ , وَ حَـجُّ بَـيْـتِ اللهِ الْـحَـرَامِ . فَـدَلِـيـلُ الـشَّـهَـادَةِ قَـوْلُـه ﴿ شَهِدَ ٱللَّهُ أَنَّهُۥ لَآ إِلَٰهَ إِلَّا هُوَ وَٱلْمَلَٰٓئِكَةُ وَأُوْلُواْ ٱلْعِلْمِ قَآئِمَۢا بِٱلْقِسْطِۚ لَآ إِلَٰهَ إِلَّا هُوَ ٱلْعَزِيزُ ٱلْحَكِيمُ ﴿١٨﴾ ﴾ وَ مَـعْـنَـاهَـا : لَا مَـعْـبُـودَ بِـحَـقٍّ إِلَّا اللهُ , (لَا إِلَـهَ) نَـافِـيـاً جَـمِـيـعَ مَـا يُـعْـبَـدُ مِـنْ دُونِ اللهِ . (إِلَّا اللهُ) مُـثْـبِـتـاً الْـعِـبَـادَةَ للهِ وَحْـدَهُ لَا شَـرِيـكَ لَـهُ فِـي عِـبَـادَتِـهِ كَـمَـا لَا شَـرِيـكَ لَـهُ فِـي مُـلْـكِـهِ . وَ تَـفْـسِـيـرُهَـا الَّـذِي يُـوَضِّـحُـهَـا , قَـوْلُـهُ تَـعَـالَـى : ﴿ وَإِذْ قَالَ إِبْرَٰهِيمُ لِأَبِيهِ وَقَوْمِهِۦٓ إِنَّنِي بَرَآءٌ

مِّمَّا تَعۡبُدُونَ ﴿٢٦﴾ إِلَّا ٱلَّذِي فَطَرَنِي فَإِنَّهُۥ سَيَهۡدِينِ ﴿٢٧﴾ وَجَعَلَهَا كَلِمَةَۢ بَاقِيَةً فِي عَقِبِهِۦ
لَعَلَّهُمۡ يَرۡجِعُونَ ﴿٢٨﴾ ﴾ وَ قَوْلُهُ : ﴿ قُلۡ يَٰٓأَهۡلَ ٱلۡكِتَٰبِ تَعَالَوۡاْ إِلَىٰ كَلِمَةٖ سَوَآءِۭ
بَيۡنَنَا وَبَيۡنَكُمۡ أَلَّا نَعۡبُدَ إِلَّا ٱللَّهَ وَلَا نُشۡرِكَ بِهِۦ شَيۡـٔٗا وَلَا يَتَّخِذَ بَعۡضُنَا بَعۡضًا أَرۡبَابٗا
مِّن دُونِ ٱللَّهِۚ فَإِن تَوَلَّوۡاْ فَقُولُواْ ٱشۡهَدُواْ بِأَنَّا مُسۡلِمُونَ ﴿٦٤﴾ ﴾ وَ دَلِيلُ
الشَّهَادَةِ أَنَّ مُحَمَّداً رَسُولُ اللهِ (صَلَّى اللهُ عَلَيْهِ وَ سَلَّمَ)
قَوْلُهُ تَعَالَى : ﴿ لَقَدۡ جَآءَكُمۡ رَسُولٞ مِّنۡ أَنفُسِكُمۡ عَزِيزٌ عَلَيۡهِ ,
مَا عَنِتُّمۡ حَرِيصٌ عَلَيۡكُم بِٱلۡمُؤۡمِنِينَ رَءُوفٞ رَّحِيمٞ ﴿١٢٨﴾ ﴾ وَ
مَعْنَى شَهَادَةِ أَنَّ مُحَمَّداً رَسُولُ اللهِ (صَلَّى اللهُ عَلَيْهِ وَ
سَلَّمَ) : طَاعَتُهُ فِيمَا أَمَرَ , وَ تَصْدِيقُهُ فِيمَا أَخْبَرَ
وَاجْتِنَابُ مَا نَهَى عَنْهُ وَ زَجَرَ , وَ أَنَّ لَا يُعْبَدُ اللهُ إِلَّا
بِمَا شَرَعَ . وَ دَلِيلُ الصَّلَاةِ وَ الزَّكَاةِ وَ تَفْسِيرُ التَّوْحِيدِ
قَوْلُهُ تَعَالَى : ﴿ وَمَآ أُمِرُوٓاْ إِلَّا لِيَعۡبُدُواْ ٱللَّهَ مُخۡلِصِينَ لَهُ ٱلدِّينَ حُنَفَآءَ وَيُقِيمُواْ
ٱلصَّلَوٰةَ وَيُؤۡتُواْ ٱلزَّكَوٰةَۚ وَذَٰلِكَ دِينُ ٱلۡقَيِّمَةِ ﴿٥﴾ ﴾ وَ دَلِيلُ الصِّيَامِ قَوْلُهُ
تَعَالَى : ﴿ يَٰٓأَيُّهَا ٱلَّذِينَ ءَامَنُواْ كُتِبَ عَلَيۡكُمُ ٱلصِّيَامُ كَمَا كُتِبَ عَلَى ٱلَّذِينَ
مِن قَبۡلِكُمۡ لَعَلَّكُمۡ تَتَّقُونَ ﴿١٨٣﴾ ﴾ وَ دَلِيلُ الْحَجِّ قَوْلُهُ تَعَالَى : ﴿

وَلِلَّهِ عَلَى ٱلنَّاسِ حِجُّ ٱلْبَيْتِ مَنِ ٱسْتَطَاعَ إِلَيْهِ سَبِيلًا ۚ وَمَن كَفَرَ فَإِنَّ ٱللَّهَ غَنِيٌّ عَنِ ٱلْعَٰلَمِينَ ﴿٩٧﴾ ﴾ الْمَرْتَبَةُ الثَّانِيَةُ : الْإِيمَانُ . وَ هُوَ بِضْعٌ وَ سَبْعُونَ شُعْبَةً , فَأَعْلَاهَا قَوْلُ (لَا إِلَهَ إِلَّا اللهُ) , وَ أَدْنَاهَا إِمَاطَةُ الْأَذَى عَنِ الطَّرِيقِ , وَ الْحَيَاءُ شُبْعَةٌ مِنَ الْإِيمَانِ . وَ أَرْكَانُهُ سِتَّةٌ : أَنْ تُؤْمِنَ بِاللهِ , وَ مَلَائِكَتِهِ , وَ كُتُبِهِ , وَ رُسُلِهِ , وَ الْيَوْمِ الْآخِرِ , وَ تُؤْمِنَ بِالْقَدَرِ خَيْرِهِ وَ شَرِّهِ . وَ الدَّلِيلُ عَلَى هَذِهِ الْأَرْكَانِ السِّتَّةِ قَوْلُهُ تَعَالَى : ﴿ ۞ لَّيْسَ ٱلْبِرَّ أَن تُوَلُّوا۟ وُجُوهَكُمْ قِبَلَ ٱلْمَشْرِقِ وَٱلْمَغْرِبِ وَلَٰكِنَّ ٱلْبِرَّ مَنْ ءَامَنَ بِٱللَّهِ وَٱلْيَوْمِ ٱلْءَاخِرِ وَٱلْمَلَٰٓئِكَةِ وَٱلْكِتَٰبِ وَٱلنَّبِيِّۦنَ ﴾ وَ دَلِيلُ الْقَدَرِ قَوْلُهُ تَعَالَى : ﴿ إِنَّا كُلَّ شَىْءٍ خَلَقْنَٰهُ بِقَدَرٍ ﴿٤٩﴾ ﴾ الْمَرْتَبَةُ الثَّالِثَةُ : (الْإِحْسَانُ) : رُكْنٌ وَاحِدٌ , وَ هُوَ أَنْ تَعْبُدَ اللهَ كَأَنَّكَ تَرَاهُ , فَإِنْ لَمْ تَكُنْ تَرَاهُ فَإِنَّهُ يَرَاكَ . وَ الدَّلِيلُ قَوْلُهُ تَعَالَى : ﴿ إِنَّ ٱللَّهَ مَعَ ٱلَّذِينَ ٱتَّقَوا۟ وَّٱلَّذِينَ هُم مُّحْسِنُونَ ﴿١٢٨﴾ ﴾ وَ قَوْلُهُ ﴿ وَتَوَكَّلْ عَلَى ٱلْعَزِيزِ ٱلرَّحِيمِ ﴿٢١٧﴾ ٱلَّذِى يَرَىٰكَ حِينَ تَقُومُ ﴿٢١٨﴾ وَتَقَلُّبَكَ فِى ٱلسَّٰجِدِينَ ﴿٢١٩﴾ إِنَّهُۥ هُوَ ٱلسَّمِيعُ ٱلْعَلِيمُ ﴿٢٢٠﴾ ﴾ وَ قَوْلُهُ تَعَالَى : ﴿ وَمَا تَكُونُ فِى شَأْنٍ وَمَا تَتْلُوا۟ مِنْهُ مِن قُرْءَانٍ

وَلَا تَعۡمَلُونَ مِنۡ عَمَلٍ إِلَّا كُنَّا عَلَيۡكُمۡ شُهُودًا إِذۡ تُفِيضُونَ فِيهِۚ ﴾ وَ الـدَّلِـيـلُ مِـنَ الـسَّـنَّـةِ : حَـدِيـثُ جِـبْـرَائِـيـلَ الْـمَـشْـهُـورِ , عَـنْ عُـمَـرَ (رَضِـيَ اللهُ عَـنْـهُ) قَـالَ : ((بَـيْـنَـمَـا نَـحْـنُ جُـلُـوسٌ عِـنْـدَ رَسُـولِ اللهِ (صَـلَّـى اللهُ عَـلَـيْـهِ وَ سَـلَّـمَ) ذَاتَ يَـوْمٍ إِذْ طَـلَـعَ عَـلَـيْـنَـا رَجُـلٌ : شَـدِيـدُ بَـيَـاضِ الـثِّـيَـابِ , شَـدِيـدُ سَـوَادِ الـشَّـعْـرِ , لَا يُـرَى عَـلَـيْـهِ أَثَـرُ الـسَّـفَـرِ, وَ لَا يَـعْـرِفُـهُ مِـنَّـا أَحَـدٌ , حَـتَّـى جَـلَـسَ إِلَـى الـنَّـبِـيِّ (صَـلَّـى اللهُ عَـلَـيْـهِ وَ سَـلَّـمَ), فَـأَسْـنَـدَ رُكْـبَـتَـيْـهِ إِلَـى رُكْـبَـتَـيْـهِ, وَ وَضَـعَ كَـفَّـيْـهِ عَـلَـى فَـخِـذَيْـهِ . وَ قَـالَ : يَـا مُـحَـمَّـدُ, أَخْـبِـرْنِـي عَـنِ الْإِسْـلَامِ ؟ فَـقَـالَ رَسُـولُ اللهِ (صَـلَّـى اللهُ عَـلَـيْـهِ وَ سَـلَّـمَ) : الْإِسْـلَامُ أَنْ تَـشْـهَـدَ أَنْ لَا إِلَـهَ إِلَّا اللهُ , وَ أَنَّ مُـحَـمَّـداً رَسُـولُ اللهِ, وَ تُـقِـيـمَ الـصَّـلَاةَ , وَ تُـؤْتِـيَ الـزَّكَـاةَ , وَ تَـصُـومَ رَمَـضَـانَ , وَ تَـحُـجَّ الْـبَـيْـتَ إِنِ اسْـتَـطَـعْـتَ إِلَـيْـهِ سَـبِـيـلاً . قَـالَ : صَـدَقْـتَ . فَـعَـجِـبْـنَـا لَـهُ يَـسْـأَلُـهُ وَ يُـصَـدِّقُـهُ . قَـالَ : فَـأَخْـبِـرْنِـي عَـنِ الْإِيـمَـانِ ؟ قَـالَ : أَنْ تُـؤْمِـنَ بِـاللهِ, وَ مَـلَائِـكَـتِـهِ, وَ كُـتُـبِـهِ , وَ رُسُـلِـهِ ,وَالْـيَـوْمِ الْآخِـرِ, وَ بِـالْـقَـدَرِ خَـيْـرِهِ وَ شَـرِّهِ. قَـالَ : صَـدَقْـتَ, قَـالَ : فَـأَخْـبِـرْنِـي عَـنِ

الْإِحْسَانِ ؟ قَالَ : أَنْ تَعْبُدَ اللهَ كَأَنَّكَ تَرَاهُ , فَإِنْ لَمْ تَكُنْ تَرَاهُ فَإِنَّهُ يَرَاكَ . قَالَ : فَأَخْبِرْنِي عَنِ السَّاعَةِ ؟ قَالَ : مَا الْمَسْئُولُ عَنْهَا بِأَعْلَمَ مِنَ السَّائِلِ !! قَالَ : أَخْبِرْنِي عَنْ أَمَارَاتِهَا ؟ قَالَ : أَنْ تَلِدَ الْأَمَةُ رَبَّتَهَا , وَ أَنْ تَرَى الْحُفَاةَ الْعُرَاةَ الْعَالَةَ رِعَاءَ الشَّاةِ يَتَطَاوَلُونَ فِي الْبُنْيَانِ . قَالَ : فَمَضَى , فَلَبِثْنَا مَلِيًّا , فَقَالَ : يَا عُمَرُ , أَ تَدْرِي مَنِ السَّائِلُ ؟ قُلْتُ : اللهُ وَ رَسُولُهُ أَعْلَمُ . قَالَ : هَذَا جِبْرِيلُ أَتَاكُمْ يُعَلِّمُكُمْ أَمْرَ دِينِكُمْ .))

الْأَصْلُ الثَّالِثُ : مَعْرِفَةُ نَبِيِّكُمْ (صَلَّى اللهُ عَلَيْهِ وَ سَلَّمَ) , وَ هُوَ مُحَمَّدُ بْنُ عَبْدِ اللهِ بْنِ عَبْدِ الْمُطَّلِبِ بْنِ هَاشِمٍ , وَ هَاشِمٌ مِنْ قُرَيْشٍ , وَ قُرَيْشٌ مِنَ الْعَرَبِ , وَ الْعَرَبُ مِنْ ذُرِّيَّةِ إِسْمَاعِيلَ بْنِ إِبْرَاهِيمَ الْخَلِيلِ , عَلَيْهِ وَ عَلَى نَبِيِّنَا أَفْضَلُ الصَّلَاةِ وَ السَّلَامِ . وَ لَهُ مِنَ الْعُمْرِ ثَلَاثٌ وَ سِتُّونَ سَنَةً , مِنْهَا أَرْبَعُونَ قَبْلَ النُّبُوَّةِ وَ ثَلَاثٌ وَ عِشْرُونَ نَبِيّاً وَ رَسُولاً . نُبِّيءَ بِـ﴿ٱقۡرَأۡ﴾ وَ أُرْسِلَ بِـ﴿ٱلۡمُدَّثِّرُ

﴾. وَ بَلَدُهُ مَكَّةُ, وَهَاجَرَ إِلَى الْمَدِينَةِ بَعَثَهُ اللهُ بِالنَّذَارَةِ عَنِ الشِّرْكِ, وَ يَدْعُو إِلَى التَّوْحِيدِ. وَالدَّلِيلُ قَوْلُهُ تَعَالَى: ﴿يَٰٓأَيُّهَا ٱلْمُدَّثِّرُ ﴿١﴾ قُمْ فَأَنذِرْ ﴿٢﴾ وَرَبَّكَ فَكَبِّرْ ﴿٣﴾ وَثِيَابَكَ فَطَهِّرْ ﴿٤﴾ وَٱلرُّجْزَ فَٱهْجُرْ ﴿٥﴾ وَلَا تَمْنُن تَسْتَكْثِرُ ﴿٦﴾ وَلِرَبِّكَ فَٱصْبِرْ ﴿٧﴾﴾ وَ مَعْنَى: ﴿قُمْ فَأَنذِرْ﴾: يُنْذِرُ عَنِ الشِّرْكِ وَ يَدْعُو إِلَى التَّوْحِيدِ. ﴿وَرَبَّكَ فَكَبِّرْ ﴿٣﴾﴾: أَيْ: عَظِّمْكَ بِالتَّوْحِيدِ. ﴿وَثِيَابَكَ فَطَهِّرْ ﴿٤﴾﴾: أَيْ: طَهِّرْ أَعْمَالَكَ عَنِ الشِّرْكِ. ﴿وَٱلرُّجْزَ فَٱهْجُرْ ﴿٥﴾﴾: الرُّجْزُ: الْأَصْنَامُ, وَ هَجْرُهَا تَرْكُهَا وَالْبَرَاءَةُ مِنْهَا وَ مِنْ أَهْلِهَا. أَخَذَ عَلَى هَذَا عَشْرَ سِنِينَ يَدْعُو إِلَى التَّوْحِيدِ. وَ بَعْدَ الْعَشْرِ عُرِجَ بِهِ إِلَى السَّمَاءِ, وَ فُرِضَتْ عَلَيْهِ الصَّلَوَاتُ الْخَمْسُ, وَ صَلَّى فِي مَكَّةَ ثَلَاثَ سِنِينَ. وَ بَعْدَهَا أُمِرَ بِالْهِجْرَةِ إِلَى الْمَدِينَةِ. وَالْهِجْرَةُ فَرِيضَةٌ عَلَى هَذِهِ الْأُمَّةِ مِنْ بَلَدِ الشِّرْكِ إِلَى بَلَدِ الْإِسْلَامِ, وَ هِيَ بَاقِيَةٌ إِلَى أَنْ تَقُومَ السَّاعَةُ. وَ الدَّلِيلُ قَوْلُهُ تَعَالَى: ﴿إِنَّ ٱلَّذِينَ تَوَفَّىٰهُمُ ٱلْمَلَٰٓئِكَةُ ظَالِمِىٓ أَنفُسِهِمْ قَالُوا۟ فِيمَ كُنتُمْ ۖ قَالُوا۟ كُنَّا مُسْتَضْعَفِينَ فِى ٱلْأَرْضِ ۚ قَالُوٓا۟ أَلَمْ تَكُنْ أَرْضُ ٱللَّهِ

وَٰسِعَةً فَتُهَاجِرُواْ فِيهَاۚ فَأُوْلَٰٓئِكَ مَأْوَىٰهُمْ جَهَنَّمُۖ وَسَآءَتْ مَصِيرًا ﴿٩٧﴾ إِلَّا ٱلْمُسْتَضْعَفِينَ مِنَ ٱلرِّجَالِ وَٱلنِّسَآءِ وَٱلْوِلْدَٰنِ لَا يَسْتَطِيعُونَ حِيلَةً وَلَا يَهْتَدُونَ سَبِيلًا ﴿٩٨﴾ فَأُوْلَٰٓئِكَ عَسَى ٱللَّهُ أَن يَعْفُوَ عَنْهُمْۚ وَكَانَ ٱللَّهُ عَفُوًّا غَفُورًا ﴿٩٩﴾ ۞ وَمَن يُهَاجِرْ فِي سَبِيلِ ٱللَّهِ يَجِدْ فِي ٱلْأَرْضِ مُرَٰغَمًا كَثِيرًا وَسَعَةًۚ وَمَن يَخْرُجْ مِنۢ بَيْتِهِۦ مُهَاجِرًا إِلَى ٱللَّهِ وَرَسُولِهِۦ ثُمَّ يُدْرِكْهُ ٱلْمَوْتُ فَقَدْ وَقَعَ أَجْرُهُۥ عَلَى ٱللَّهِۗ وَكَانَ ٱللَّهُ غَفُورًا رَّحِيمًا ﴿١٠٠﴾ ﴾ وَ قَوْلُهُ تَعَالَى : ﴿ يَٰعِبَادِيَ ٱلَّذِينَ ءَامَنُوٓاْ إِنَّ أَرْضِي وَٰسِعَةٌ فَإِيَّٰيَ فَٱعْبُدُونِ ﴿٥٦﴾ ﴾ قَالَ الْبَغَوِيُّ - رَحِمَهُ اللهُ تَعَالَى- : ((سَبَبُ نُزُولِ هَذِهِ الْآيَةِ فِي الْمُسْلِمِينَ الَّذِينَ بِمَكَّةَ : لَمْ يُهَاجِرُوا , نَادَاهُمُ اللهُ بِاسْمِ الْإِيمَانِ)). وَ الدَّلِيلُ عَلَى الْهِجْرَةِ مِنَ السُّنَّةِ قَوْلُهُ (صَلَّى اللهُ عَلَيْهِ وَ سَلَّمَ) : ((لَا تَنْقَطِعُ الْهِجْرَةُ حَتَّى تَنْقَطِعَ التَّوْبَةُ , وَ لَا تَنْقَطِعُ التَّوْبَةُ حَتَّى تَطْلُعَ الشَّمْسُ مِنْ مَغْرِبِهَا)). فَلَمَّا اسْتَقَرَّ فِي الْمَدِينَةِ أُمِرَ بِبَقِيَّةِ شَرَائِعِ الْإِسْلَامِ مِثْلَ الزَّكَاةِ , وَالصَّوْمِ , وَ الْحَجِّ , وَ الْأَذَانِ , وَ الْجِهَادِ , وَالْأَمْرِ بِالْمَعْرُوفِ , وَ النَّهْيِ عَنِ الْمُنْكَرِ , وَ غَيْرِ ذَلِكَ مِنْ شَرَائِعِ الْإِسْلَامِ . أَخَذَ عَلَى هَذَا عَشْرَ

سِنِينَ , ثُمَّ تُوفِيَ - صَلَوَاتُ اللهِ وَ سَلَامُهُ عَلَيْهِ - وَ دِينُهُ بَاقٍ , وَ هَذَا دِينُهُ لَا خَيْرَ إِلَّا دَلَّ الْأُمَّةَ عَلَيْهِ وَ لَا شَرَّ إِلَّا حَذَّرَ مِنْهُ, وَالْخَيْرُ الَّذِي دَلَّ عَلَيْهِ: التَّوْحِيدُ وَ جَمِيعُ مَا يُحِبُّهُ اللهُ وَ يَرْضَاهُ , وَ الشَّرُّ الَّذِي حَذَرَهَا مِنْهُ : الشِّرْكُ وَ جَمِيعُ مَا يَكْرَهُهُ اللهُ وَ يَأْبَاهُ. بَعَثَهُ اللهُ إِلَى النَّاسِ كَافَّةً, وَافْتَرَضَ طَاعَتَهُ عَلَى جَمِيعِ الثَّقَلَيْنِ - الْجِنِّ وَ الْإِنْسِ - , وَ الدَّلِيلُ قَوْلُهُ تَعَالَى: ﴿ قُلْ يَٰٓأَيُّهَا ٱلنَّاسُ إِنِّي رَسُولُ ٱللَّهِ إِلَيْكُمْ جَمِيعًا ﴾ وَ أَكْمَلَ اللهُ بِهِ الدِّينَ , وَ الدَّلِيلُ قَوْلُهُ تَعَالَى : ﴿ ٱلْيَوْمَ أَكْمَلْتُ لَكُمْ دِينَكُمْ وَأَتْمَمْتُ عَلَيْكُمْ نِعْمَتِي وَرَضِيتُ لَكُمُ ٱلْإِسْلَٰمَ دِينًا ﴾ وَ الدَّلِيلُ عَلَى مَوْتِهِ (صَلَّى اللهُ عَلَيْهِ وَ سَلَّمَ) قَوْلُهُ تَعَالَى : ﴿ إِنَّكَ مَيِّتٌ وَإِنَّهُم مَّيِّتُونَ ﴿٣٠﴾ ثُمَّ إِنَّكُمْ يَوْمَ ٱلْقِيَٰمَةِ عِندَ رَبِّكُمْ تَخْتَصِمُونَ ﴿٣١﴾ ﴾ وَالنَّاسُ إِذَا مَاتُوا يُبْعَثُونَ , وَ الدَّلِيلُ قَوْلُهُ تَعَالَى : ﴿ ۞ مِنْهَا خَلَقْنَٰكُمْ وَفِيهَا نُعِيدُكُمْ وَمِنْهَا نُخْرِجُكُمْ تَارَةً أُخْرَىٰ ﴿٥٥﴾ ﴾ وَ قَوْلُهُ تَعَالَى : ﴿ وَٱللَّهُ أَنۢبَتَكُم مِّنَ ٱلْأَرْضِ نَبَاتًا ﴿١٧﴾ ثُمَّ يُعِيدُكُمْ فِيهَا وَيُخْرِجُكُمْ إِخْرَاجًا ﴿١٨﴾ ﴾ وَ بَعْدَ الْبَعْثِ مُحَاسَبُونَ , وَ

مَـجْـزِيُـونَ بِـأَعْـمَـالِـهِـمْ , وَ الـدَّلِـيـلُ قَـوْلُـهُ تَـعَـالَـى : ﴿لِيَجْزِيَ ٱلَّذِينَ أَسَٰٓـُٔواْ بِمَا عَمِلُواْ وَيَجْزِيَ ٱلَّذِينَ أَحْسَنُواْ بِٱلْحُسْنَى ﴿٣١﴾﴾ وَ مَـنْ كَـذَّبَ بِـالْـبَـعْـثِ بَـعْـدَ الْـمَـوْتِ كَـفَـرَ. وَ الـدَّلِـيـلُ قَـوْلُـهُ تَـعَـالَـى : ﴿زَعَمَ ٱلَّذِينَ كَفَرُوٓاْ أَن لَّن يُبْعَثُواْۚ قُلْ بَلَىٰ وَرَبِّي لَتُبْعَثُنَّ ثُمَّ لَتُنَبَّؤُنَّ بِمَا عَمِلْتُمْۚ وَذَٰلِكَ عَلَى ٱللَّهِ يَسِيرٌ ﴿٧﴾﴾ وَ أَرْسَـلَ جَـمِـيـعَ الـرُّسُـلِ مُـبَـشِّـرِيـنَ وَ مُـنْـذِرِيـنَ , وَ الـدَّلِـيـلُ قَـوْلُـهُ تَـعَـالَـى : ﴿رُّسُلٗا مُّبَشِّرِينَ وَمُنذِرِينَ لِئَلَّا يَكُونَ لِلنَّاسِ عَلَى ٱللَّهِ حُجَّةُۢ بَعْدَ ٱلرُّسُلِۚ﴾ وَ أَوَّلُـهُـمْ نُـوحٌ (عَـلَـيْـهِ الـسَّـلَام) , وَ آخِـرُهُـمْ مُـحَـمَّـدٌ (صَـلَّـى اللهُ عَـلَـيْـهِ وَ سَـلَّـمَ) مُـحَـمَّـدٌ (صَـلَّـى اللهُ عَـلَـيْـهِ وَ سَـلَّـمَ) خَـاتَـمُ الـنَّـبِـيِّـيـنَ. وَ الـدَّلِـيـلُ عَـلَـى أَنَّ أَوَّلَـهُـمْ نُـوحٌ قَـوْلُـهُ تَـعَـالَـى : ﴿۞ إِنَّآ أَوْحَيْنَآ إِلَيْكَ كَمَآ أَوْحَيْنَآ إِلَىٰ نُوحٖ وَٱلنَّبِيِّـۧنَ مِنۢ بَعْدِهِۦۚ﴾. وَ كُـلُّ أُمَّـةٍ بَـعَـثَ اللهُ إِلَـيْـهَـا رَسُـولاً مِـنْ نُـوحٍ إِلَـى مُـحَـمَّـدٍ (صَـلَّـى اللهُ عَـلَـيْـهِ وَ سَـلَّـمَ) يَـأْمُـرُهُـمْ بِـعِـبَـادَةِ اللهِ وَحْـدَهُ, وَ يَـنْـهَـاهُـمْ عَـنْ عِـبَـادَةِ الـطَّـاغُـوتِ. وَ الـدَّلِـيـلُ قَـوْلُـهُ تَـعَـالَـى : ﴿وَلَقَدْ بَعَثْنَا فِي كُلِّ أُمَّةٖ رَّسُولًا أَنِ ٱعْبُدُواْ ٱللَّهَ وَٱجْتَنِبُواْ ٱلطَّٰغُوتَۖ﴾ وَ افْـتَـرَضَ اللهُ عَـلَـى جَـمِـيـعِ الْـعِـبَـادِ الْـكُـفْـرَ

بِالطَّاغُوتِ, وَالإِيْمَانُ بِاللهِ . قَالَ ابْنُ الْقَيِّمِ - رَحِمَهُ اللهُ تَعَالَى - : (مَعْنَى (الطَّاغُوتِ) : مَا تَجَاوَزَ بِهِ الْعَبْدُ حَدَّهُ مِنْ مَعْبُودٍ أَوْ مَتْبُوعٍ أَوْ مُطَاعٍ)). وَالطَّوَاغِيتُ كَثِيرَةٌ رُؤُوسُهُمْ خَمْسَةٌ : إِبْلِيسُ لَعَنَهُ اللهُ , وَمَنْ عُبِدَ وَهُوَ رَاضٍ وَ مَنْ دَعَا النَّاسَ إِلَى عِبَادَةِ نَفْسِهِ وَ مَنْ دُعِيَ شَيْئًا مِنْ عِلْمِ الْغَيْبِ وَ مَنْ حَكَمَ بِغَيْرِ مَا أَنْزَلَ اللهُ , وَالدَّلِيلُ قَوْلُهُ تَعَالَى : ﴿لَآ إِكۡرَاهَ فِي ٱلدِّينِۖ قَد تَّبَيَّنَ ٱلرُّشۡدُ مِنَ ٱلۡغَيِّۚ فَمَن يَكۡفُرۡ بِٱلطَّٰغُوتِ وَيُؤۡمِنۢ بِٱللَّهِ فَقَدِ ٱسۡتَمۡسَكَ بِٱلۡعُرۡوَةِ ٱلۡوُثۡقَىٰ لَا ٱنفِصَامَ لَهَاۗ وَٱللَّهُ سَمِيعٌ عَلِيمٌ ٢٥٦﴾ وَ هَذَا مَعْنَى لَا إِلَهَ إِلَّا اللهُ. وَ فِي الْحَدِيثِ : ((رَأْسُ الْأَمْرِ الْإِسْلَامِ , وَعَمُودُهُ الصَّلَاةُ , وَ ذِرْوَةُ سَنَامِهِ الْجِهَادُ فِي سَبِيلِ اللهِ)), وَ اللهُ أَعْلَمُ. وَ صَلَّى اللهُ عَلَى نَبِيِّنَا مَحَمَّدٍ, وَ عَلَى آلِهِ وَ صَحْبِهِ وَ سَلَّمَ.

TRANSLITERATION TABLE

Consonants

ء	ʾ	د	d	ض	ḍ	ك	k
ب	b	ذ	dh	ط	ṭ	ل	l
ت	t	ر	r	ظ	ẓ	م	m
ث	th	ز	z	ع	ʿ	ن	n
ج	j	س	s	غ	gh	هـ	h
ح	ḥ	ش	sh	ف	f	و	w
خ	kh	ص	ṣ	ق	q	ي	y

Vowels

Short	ـَ	a	ـِ	i	ـُ	u
Long	ـَا	ā	ـِي	ī	ـُو	ū
Diphthongs	ـَوْ	aw	ـَيْ	ay		

Arabic Symbols & their meanings

عَزَّ وَجَلَّ	سُبْحَانَهُ وَتَعَالَى	رَحِمَهُ ٱللَّهُ	حَفِظَهُ اللهُ
(Allāh) the Mighty & Sublime	Glorified & Exalted is Allāh	May Allāh have mercy on him	May Allāh preserve him
صَلَّى ٱللَّهُ عَلَيْهِ وَعَلَىٰ آلِهِ وَسَلَّمَ	جَلَّ جَلَالُهُ	جَلَّ وَعَلَا	تَبَارَكَ وَتَعَالَى
May Allāh elevate his rank & grant him peace	(Allāh) His Majesty is Exalted	(Allāh) the Sublime & Exalted	(Allāh) the Blessed & Exalted
رَضِيَ ٱللَّهُ عَنْهُمْ	رَضِيَ ٱللَّهُ عَنْهَا	رَضِيَ ٱللَّهُ عَنْهُ	عَلَيْهِ ٱلصَّلَاةُ وَٱلسَّلَامُ
May Allāh be pleased with them	May Allāh be pleased with her	May Allāh be pleased with him	May Allāh elevate his rank & grant him peace
			رَحِمَهُمُ ٱللَّهُ
			May Allāh have mercy upon them

THE EXPLAINER'S INTRODUCTION OF THE THREE FUNDAMENTAL PRINCIPLES AND ITS AUTHOR

This is an important message of belief written by Shaykh Abū ʿAbdullāh Muḥammad Bin ʿAbdul Wahhāb Bin Sulaymān Bin ʿAli At-Tamīmī Al-Hanbali famous Imām and reviver for the false symbols (attached) to Islām in the second half of the twelve century , may Allāh have mercy on him and bestow upon him an abode (in Paradise). ī

he used to teach the students and the public these fundamental principles. In turn they would study and memorize these principles to be so it will be firmly embedded in their hearts because this matter is a basic principle in ʿAqīdah.

He died 1206 on the Islāmic calendar and was born 1115 on the Islāmic calendar. He lived 91 years of which it was filled with good, the calling to the religion of Allāh, teaching, and advising, and enduring (harm) in that.

Allāh utilized him as a means for saving the servants and countries in the Arabian Peninsula during his life.. Those callers who took knowledge from him and carried it to other countries was the reason why his Dawah spread in Syria, Egypt, Iraq, India, and other places.

His Dawah was also propagated through letters, books, the Shaykh's adherents, supporters, and callers that followed him in the call to Allāh..

EXPLANATION OF THE AUTHOR'S INTRODUCTION

Shaykh ul-Islām Muḥammad bin ʿAbdul-Wahhāb (رَحِمَهُ ٱللَّهُ) said,

اِعْلَمْ - رَحِمَكَ اللهُ - أَنَّهُ يَجِبُ عَلَيْنَا تَعَلُّمُ أَرْبَعِ مَسَائِلَ, اَلْأُولَى: اَلْعِلْمُ وَ هُوَ مَعْرِفَةُ اللهِ, وَمَعْرِفَةُ نَبِيِّهِ, وَ مَعْرِفَةُ دِينِ الْإِسْلَامِ بِالْأَدِلَّةِ. اَلثَّانِيَةُ: اَلْعَمَلُ بِهِ اَلثَّالِثَةُ: الدَّعْوَةُ إِلَيْهِ. اَلرَّابِعَةُ: اَلصَّبْرُ عَلَى الْأَذَى فِيهِ. وَالدَّلِيلُ قَوْلُهُ تَعَالَى: ﴿وَٱلْعَصْرِ ١ إِنَّ ٱلْإِنسَٰنَ لَفِى خُسْرٍ ٢ إِلَّا ٱلَّذِينَ ءَامَنُوا۟ وَعَمِلُوا۟ ٱلصَّٰلِحَٰتِ وَتَوَاصَوْا۟ بِٱلْحَقِّ وَتَوَاصَوْا۟ بِٱلصَّبْرِ ٣﴾ [العصر: ١ – ٣]. قَالَ الشَّافِعِي - رَحِمَهُ اللهُ -: لَوْ مَا أَنْزَلَ اللهُ حُجَّةً عَلَى

خَـلْـقِـهِ إِلَّا هَـذِهِ الـسُّـورَةَ لَـكَـفَـتْـهُـمْ وَ قَـالَ الْـبُـخَـارِي - رَحِـمَـهُ اللهُ تَـعَـالَـى - : بَـابُ الْـعِـلْـمِ قَـبْـلَ الْـقَـوْلِ وَ الْـعَـمَـلِ . وَ الـدَّلِـيـلُ : ﴿ فَٱعۡلَمۡ أَنَّهُۥ لَآ إِلَٰهَ إِلَّا ٱللَّهُ وَٱسۡتَغۡفِرۡ لِذَنۢبِكَ ﴾ [محمد: ١٩] . فَـبَـدَأَ بِـالْـعِـلْـمِ قَـبْـلَ الْـقَـوْلِ وَ الْـعَـمَـلِ

"Know, may Allāh have mercy on you, that it is obligatory upon us to learn four matters:

The First is knowledge which is knowing Allāh, knowing His Messenger, and knowing the religion of Islām with proofs. The Second is to implement this knowledge. The Third is Propagating this knowledge. the Forth is enduring the harm faced in it..

The evidence to (these four matters) is the saying of Allāh (سُبۡحَانَهُۥ وَتَعَالَىٰ),

"By Al-'Asr (the time) Verily! Man is in loss. Except those who believe and do righteous good deeds, and recommend one another to the truth and recommend one another to patience." [Sūrah 'Asr 103:1-3]

Al-Shāfī said – (رَحِمَهُ ٱللَّهُ)- "Had Allāh only sent this Sūrah as a proof (for or against) mankind it would be sufficient (for them).."

Al-Bukhārī (رَحِمَهُ ٱللَّهُ) said, "Chapter on Knowledge proceeds statements and actions" and the proof for that is found in Allāh's (سُبْحَانَهُ وَتَعَالَىٰ) statement : "So know (O Muḥammad صَلَّى ٱللَّهُ عَلَيْهِ وَسَلَّمَ) that La ilaha ill-Allāh (none has the right to be worshipped but Allāh), and ask forgiveness for your sin." [Sūrah Muḥammad 47:19]

So, He started with knowledge before statements and actions."

Explanation

These matters require from the believing man and woman, young and old to learn.

The author (رَحِمَهُ ٱللَّهُ) said,

الأُولَى : الْعِلْمُ

"The first is: knowledge" one is obliged to learn and gain insight so that he will upon clarity. He must learn about the religion of Allāh which he was created for. This knowledge is learning about Allāh, His Prophet, and the religion of Islām with proofs.

So, that is the first matter that the servant gains insight about who is his Lord?

Hence, he learns that his Lord is the Creator who created him, provides his subsistence, and confers His favors upon him. Allāh created those who came before him, and those who will come after him. He is the Lord of all that exists. Allāh is the one true deity and object of servitude. no one besides Him deserves to be worshiped. Not a close angel, a messenger who was sent, not a Jinn, no human, no idol or anything else deserves to be worshiped; Rather, true worship is a right that belongs to Him alone. He is the sole object of worship in truth (سُبْحَانَهُ وَتَعَالَىٰ).

He deserved to be worshipped. He is the Lord of all that exists. He is your Lord and Master, your Creator, and your true Deity (سُبْحَانَهُ وَتَعَالَىٰ). So, you should know this first matter which is knowing your Lord, your Prophet, and your religion with proof. It is what Allāh says and his Prophet said, not by opinions and statements of so and so person. Instead it is with proofs from the verses of the Qur᾽ān and Ḥadīth. This is the religion of Islām that you have been obliged to enter and commit to.

It is the worship of Allāh which He (سُبۡحَانَهُۥ وَتَعَالَىٰ) says about it,

﴿ وَمَا خَلَقۡتُ ٱلۡجِنَّ وَٱلۡإِنسَ إِلَّا لِيَعۡبُدُونِ ﴾ ٥٦

"And I (Allāh) created not the jinn's and humans except they should worship Me (Alone." [*Sūrah Adh-Dhariyat* 51:56]

This worship is Islām. It is obeying Allāh and his Messenger. It is establishing Allāh's orders and abandoning forbidden matters.

This is the worship in which mankind was created for. Allāh orders this within His statement,

﴿ يَٰٓأَيُّهَا ٱلنَّاسُ ٱعۡبُدُواْ رَبَّكُمُ ﴾

"O mankind! Worship your Lord (Allāh)." [*Sūrah Al-Baqarah* 2:21]

Meaning: worship Him by obeying His commands and abandon His prohibitions, and submit oneself direct to him, and specify worship for Him (سُبۡحَانَهُۥوَتَعَالَىٰ).

The author (رَحِمَهُ ٱللَّهُ) said,

الْأَوَّلُ : الْعِلْمُ**"The first is knowledge"** one is obliged to learn and gain insight so that he is upon clarity. He must learn about the religion of Allāh which he was created for. This knowledge is learning about Allāh, His Prophet, and the religion of Islām with proofs.

So, that is the first matter that the servant gains insight about who is his Lord?

Hence, he learns that his Lord is the Creator who created him, provides his subsistence, and confers His favors upon him. Allāh created those who came before him and those who will come after him. He is the Lord of all that exists. Allāh is the one true deity and object of servitude. No one besides Him deserves to be worshiped. Not a close angel, a messenger who was sent, not a Jinn, no human, no idol or anything else deserves to be worshiped; Rather, true worship is a right that belongs to Him alone. He is the sole object of worship in truth (سُبۡحَانَهُۥوَتَعَالَىٰ).

He deserved to be worshipped. He is the Lord of all that exists. He is your Lord and Master, your Creator, and your true Deity (سُبۡحَانَهُۥوَتَعَالَىٰ). So, you should know this first matter which is knowing your Lord, your Prophet, and your religion with proof. It is what Allāh says, and his Prophet said, not by opinions and statements of so and so person. Instead, it is with proofs from the verses of the Qur᾿ān and Ḥadīth. This is the religion of Islām that you have been obliged to enter and commit to.

It is the worship of Allāh which He (سُبۡحَانَهُۥوَتَعَالَىٰ) says about it,

﴿ وَمَا خَلَقۡتُ ٱلۡجِنَّ وَٱلۡإِنسَ إِلَّا لِيَعۡبُدُونِ ٥٦ ﴾

> **"And I (Allāh) created not the jinn's and humans except they should worship Me (Alone."** [*Sūrah Adh-Dhariyat* 51:56]

This worship is Islām. It is obeying Allāh and His Messenger. It is establishing Allāh's orders and abandoning forbidden matters.

This is the worship in which mankind was created for. Allāh orders this within His statement,

﴿ يَٰٓأَيُّهَا ٱلنَّاسُ ٱعۡبُدُواْ رَبَّكُمُ ﴾

"O mankind! Worship your Lord (Allāh)." [*Sūrah Al-Baqarah* 2:21]

Meaning: worship Him by obeying His commands and abandon His prohibitions, and submit oneself directly to him, and specify worship for Him (سُبْحَانَهُ وَتَعَالَىٰ).

From that (knowledge) is to learn about your prophet. His full name is Muḥammad Ibn ʻAbdullāh Ibn ʻAbdul-Muttalib Al-Hāshimī Al-Qureshi al-Makki, then al-Madanī may Allāh raise his rank and grant him peace. So, you should understand that he is your Prophet whom Allāh has sent to you with the true religion, teaching you and giving you guidance. Likewise, you must believe that he is, in reality, the messenger of Allāh; that Allāh sent him to all of creation from the jinn and mankind. Adherence to him and pursuance of his methodology is a religious obligation. Which its details will come in the third fundamental principle.

The author (رَحِمَهُ ٱللَّهُ) said,

الثَّانِيَةُ :الْعَمَلُ بِهِ

"The Second - is to implement this knowledge" meaning: to act upon this religion by way of praying, fasting, striving

, Hajj, faith, Taqwā. So, implement the religion of Islām, because you are a creation of Allāh and created to worship Him.

-Learning the religion of Allāh and act upon it is a religious duty placed upon you. So, worship Allāh alone, perform prayer, pay the Zakat,{ fast Ramaḍān, perform Hajj, believe in Allāh, His angels, his Messengers, His Books, the last day, the divine decree (the good and the bad), order the good and forbid the evil, obey your parents, maintain ties with your relatives and so forth. So, carry out Allāh's commands and abstain from His prohibition, abandon acts of disobedience you have forbidden from, and carry out the obligations you have been ordered with..

The author (رَحِمَهُ ٱللَّهُ) said,

الثَّالِثَةُ : الدَّعْوَةُ إِلَيْهِ

"The Third is Propagating this knowledge " meaning that you call to this religion. So, advise the people to be upright upon the religion and give right guidance. Order them with the good and forbid evil. This is propagating the religion of Islām. Propagating the religion of Allāh according to one's knowledge and ability is a religious duty upon every Muslim.. **Therefore, a portion of this duty to convey and**

sincerely advise to this religion has been placed upon every Muslim, male and female..

One must call to the oneness of Allāh, the Ṣalāh and its preservation, the Zakat and its fulfillment, the fasting, the Hajj according to one's ability, dutifulness to one's parents, maintaining ties of kinship, and abandoning all acts of disobedience.

The author (رَحِمَهُ ٱللَّهُ) said,

الرَّابِعَةُ : الصَّبْرُ عَلَى الْأَذَى فِيهِ

"the Forth – is enduring the harm faced in it." One must endure the harm concerning these matters. Harm will occur to him. He may become weary of the one he is calling (to the religion) or others from his family. So, having patience and anticipating a reward from Allāh is a must.

So, the believer must have patience in believing in Allāh, carrying out what Allāh has ordered, leaving off what Allāh has forbidden, in calling to Allāh's religion, teaching, commanding the good and forbidding the evil.

All of these matters require patience. All aspects of the religion require patience. It requires patience in calling to

Allāh's religion, performing Ṣalāh, Zakat, fasting, Hajj, commanding the good and forbidding evil, and abstaining from impermissible acts and sins. Thus, be careful getting near them (unlawful matters & sins) as if one cannot have patience one will fall upon sin or abandon obligatory duties. , For this reason Allāh says to his Messenger,

﴿ فَٱصْبِرْ كَمَا صَبَرَ أُوْلُواْ ٱلْعَزْمِ مِنَ ٱلرُّسُلِ ﴾

"Therefore, be patient (O Muḥammad ﷺ) as did the Messengers of strong will." [*Sūrah al-Ahqāf* 46:35]

And He (سُبۡحَانَهُۥوَتَعَالَىٰ) says,

﴿ وَٱصْبِرْ لِحُكْمِ رَبِّكَ فَإِنَّكَ بِأَعْيُنِنَا ﴾

"So, wait patiently (O Muḥammad ﷺ) for the Decision of your Lord, for verily, you are under Our Eyes." [*Sūrah at-Tur* 52:48]

And He says,

﴿ وَٱصْبِرْ وَمَا صَبْرُكَ إِلَّا بِٱللَّهِ ﴾

"And endure you patiently (O Muḥammad صَلَّى ٱللَّهُ عَلَيْهِ وَسَلَّمَ), your patience is not but from Allāh." [*Sūrah an-Nahl* 16:127]

And He (سُبْحَانَهُ وَتَعَالَىٰ) says,

﴿ إِنَّمَا يُوَفَّى ٱلصَّٰبِرُونَ أَجْرَهُم بِغَيْرِ حِسَابٍ ﴿١٠﴾ ﴾

"Only those who are patient shall receive their rewards in full, without reckoning." [*Sūrah Az-Zumar* 39:10]

and He (سُبْحَانَهُ وَتَعَالَىٰ) says,

﴿ وَٱصْبِرُوٓا۟ إِنَّ ٱللَّهَ مَعَ ٱلصَّٰبِرِينَ ﴿٤٦﴾ ﴾

"Allāh is with those who are As-Sābirīn (the patient ones, etc.)." [*Sūrah Al-Anfal* 8:46]

Meaning, have patience on obeying Allāh, abandoning acts of obedience, and be wary of going against his orders and committing prohibited acts.

The proof for these four matters is what Allāh (سُبْحَانَهُ وَتَعَالَىٰ) says in Sūrah 'Asr,

﴿ وَٱلۡعَصۡرِ ١ إِنَّ ٱلۡإِنسَٰنَ لَفِي خُسۡرٍ ٢ إِلَّا ٱلَّذِينَ
ءَامَنُواْ وَعَمِلُواْ ٱلصَّٰلِحَٰتِ وَتَوَاصَوۡاْ بِٱلۡحَقِّ وَتَوَاصَوۡاْ
بِٱلصَّبۡرِ ٣ ﴾

"By Al-'Asr (the time). Verily! Man is in loss. Except those who believe and do righteous good deeds, and recommend one another to the truth and recommend one another to patience." [*Sūrah al-'Asr* 103:1-3]

This tremendous Sūrah contains a Hujjah (evidence for or against you) pertaining these aforementioned matters which encompassed the religion in totality. All of the religion consists of ʾĪmān, action, Dawah, and patience..

Believing in the truth, implementing it, calling to it, and patience on the harm that one faces. All of mankind is in ruin,

﴿ إِلَّا ٱلَّذِينَ ءَامَنُواْ وَعَمِلُواْ ٱلصَّٰلِحَٰتِ وَتَوَاصَوۡاْ بِٱلۡحَقِّ
وَتَوَاصَوۡاْ بِٱلصَّبۡرِ ٣ ﴾

"Except those who believe and do righteous good deeds, and recommend one another to the truth and recommend one another to patience."

In this verse Allāh has made these individuals the exception (to those in lost). Thus, all of humanity is in ruin and on a path headed for destruction except those who believe, do righteous deeds, recommended one another with good and patience.

They are the one who are winners happy in which Allāh swore by this in saying and He is the most truthful: **"By 'Asr"**. Even if Allāh didn't swear by 'Asr one of the purposes for doing so would be to emphasize the subject matter.

Allāh swears by whatever He wants from his creations, and none can prevent Him.

Allāh has sworn by the heaven filled with stars, the sky and the big star, the sun and its brightness, the night as it conceals, those angels who pull out the souls and so forth.

All of the creation attests to Allāh's greatness and that He is deserving of worship. He swears by these things to make apparent the great matter of this creation which attest to His Oneness and worthiness of being worshiped alone.

On the other hand, the creation can only swear by Allāh. Therefore, one must only swear and make oaths by Allāh. It is impermissible to make an oath by the Prophets, idols, the righteous, trust, the Ka'bah, or the other than that.

Based upon the statement of the Prophet (صَلَّىٱللَّهُعَلَيْهِوَسَلَّمَ) this matter becomes obligatory upon the Muslim,

مَنْ حَلَفَ بِشَيْءٍ دُونَ اللهِ فَقَدْ أَشْرَكَ

"Whoever swears by other than Allāh he has associated a partner with Allāh."[1]

He (عَلَيْهِٱلصَّلَاةُوَٱلسَّلَامُ) also said:

مَنْ كَانَ حَالِفًا فَلْيَحْلِفْ بِاللهِ أَوْ لِيَصْمُتْ

[1] Collected by Imām 'Aḥmad No. (1/47, 2/34) in his Musnad; and collected by Abū Dawūd No. (3251) and at-Tirmidhi No. (1535).

"So, whoever must take an oath, he should swear by Allāh or keep quiet." [2]

So, it is obligatory on every Muslim, male and female, to be careful of taking oaths with other than Allāh and that they make their oaths for completely for Allāh alone.

The author (رَحِمَهُ ٱللَّهُ) said,

يَقُولُ الشَّافِعِيُّ رَحِمَهُ اللهُ

"Ash-Shāfī (May Allāh have mercy upon him) said,"-and he is one of the well-known four Imāms, Muḥammad bin 'Idrīs ash-Shāfī al-Mutalibi who was born in the year 150 AH and died in the year 204 AH.

لَوْ مَا أَنْزَلَ اللهُ حُجَّةً عَلَى خَلْقِهِ إِلَّا هَذِهِ السُّورَةِ لَكَفَتْهُمْ

"If no argument besides this verse had been revealed by Allāh to his creatures, it would have been sufficient for them."

And in another version,

---

[2] It is mutually agreed upon between al-Bukhārī No. (6646) and Muslim No. (2679) from the Ḥadīth of Ibn 'Umar (رَضِيَ ٱللَّهُ عَنْهُمَا).

لَوْ فَكَّرَ النَّاسُ فِي هَذِهِ السُّورَةِ لَكَفَتْهُمْ

"if people were to contemplate over this Sūrah it would have been enough for them." [3]

Meaning: if they were to study and concentrate on this Sūrah it would have been enough for them to remain on the truth, establish what Allāh orders, and abandon unlawful matters.., Allāh explained that those who believe, do righteous good deeds, and recommend one another to the truth and . They are the winners while everyone are the losers.

This is a well-established evidence showing the obligation of mutually ordering and advising, having belief, having patience, and being truthful. The only path to happiness and winning is by these four characteristics which are sincere belief in Allāh and His Messenger, righteous deeds, mutual advisement of the truth and patience..

The author (رَحِمَهُ ٱللَّهُ) said,

قَالَ الْبُخَارِي

[3] Refer back to the book *Sīra 'Allām an-Nubulā* (8/379) in his biography No. (1539).

"And Al-Bukhārī said" full name is Abū ʿAbdullāh Muḥammad ibn Ismael ibn Ibrāhīm Al-Bukhārī, who is from Bukhārī in the Far East. He was born in 194 AH in the middle of the second century, and died 256 AH in the middle of the third century. He was 62 years old- when he died- and is the author of the "Saḥīḥ" and he has other great beneficial books.

He said in his "Saḥīḥ"[4] chapter: knowledge before statements and action based upon the statement of Allāh (سُبۡحَانَهُۥوَتَعَالَىٰ),

﴿ فَٱعۡلَمۡ أَنَّهُۥ لَآ إِلَٰهَ إِلَّا ٱللَّهُ وَٱسۡتَغۡفِرۡ لِذَنۢبِكَ ﴾

> **"So, know (O Muḥammad صَلَّىٱللَّهُعَلَيۡهِوَسَلَّمَ) that *La ilaha ill-Allah* (none has the right to be worshipped but Allah), and ask forgiveness for your sin."** [*Sūrah Muḥammad* 47:19]

So, He began with knowledge before statements and actions. So one must learn first, then implement that

[4] Refer back to Ṣaḥīḥ al-Bukhārī under *Kitaab al-Ilm* in the third book in the Ṣaḥīḥ chapter 10 between the No. (67-68).

knowledge. Thus, one should learn his religion first then implement it upon insight,

and Allāh knows best.

INTRODUCTION OF THE FIRST FUNDAMENTAL

Shaykh ul-Islām Muḥammad bin ʿAbdul-Wahhāb (رَحِمَهُ ٱللَّهُ) said,

اِعْلَمْ - رَحِمَكَ اللهُ – أَنَّهُ يَجِبُ عَلَى كُلِّ مُسْلِمٍ وَ مُسْلِمَةٍ تَعَلُّمُ ثَلَاثِ هَذِهِ الْمَسَائِلِ وَ الْعَمَلُ بِهِنَّ . اَلْأُولَى : أَنَّ اللهَ خَلَقَنَا وَ رَزَقَنَا , وَ لَمْ يَتْرُكْنَا هَمَلاً . بَلْ أَرْسَلَ إِلَيْنَا رَسُولاً . فَمَنْ أَطَاعَهُ دَخَلَ الْجَنَّةَ , وَ مَنْ عَصَاهُ دَخَلَ النَّارَ . وَالدَّلِيلُ قَوْلُهُ تَعَالَى : ﴿ إِنَّآ أَرۡسَلۡنَآ إِلَيۡكُمۡ رَسُولٗا شَٰهِدًا عَلَيۡكُمۡ كَمَآ أَرۡسَلۡنَآ إِلَىٰ فِرۡعَوۡنَ رَسُولٗا ﴿١٥﴾ فَعَصَىٰ فِرۡعَوۡنُ ٱلرَّسُولَ فَأَخَذۡنَٰهُ أَخۡذٗا وَبِيلٗا ﴿١٦﴾ ﴾ [المزمل: ١٥ –

١٦]. اَلـثَّـانِـيَـةُ : أَنَّ اللهَ لَا يَـرْضَى أَنْ يُـشْـرَكَ مَـعَـهُ أَحَـدٌ فِـي عِـبَـادَتِـهِ , لَا مَـلَـكٌ مُـقَـرَّبٌ وَ لَا نَـبِـيٌّ مُـرْسَـلٌ . وَ الـدَّلِـيـلُ قَـوْلُـهُ تَـعَـالَـى : ﴿وَأَنَّ ٱلْمَسَـٰجِدَ لِلَّهِ فَلَا تَدْعُواْ مَعَ ٱللَّهِ أَحَدًا ﴿١٨﴾﴾ [الجن: ١٨]. اَلـثَّـالِـثَـةُ : أَنَّ مَـنْ أَطَـاعَ الـرَّسُـولَ , وَ وَحَّـدَ اللهَ , لَا يَـجُـوزُ لَـهُ مُـوَالَاةُ مَـنْ حَـادَّ اللهَ وَ رَسُـولَـهُ وَ لَـوْ كَـانَ أَقْـرَبَ قَـرِيـبٍ وَ الـدَّلِـيـلُ قَـوْلُـهُ تَـعَـالَـى : ﴿لَّا تَجِدُ قَوْمًا يُؤْمِنُونَ بِٱللَّهِ وَٱلْيَوْمِ ٱلْـَٔاخِرِ يُوَآدُّونَ مَنْ حَآدَّ ٱللَّهَ وَرَسُولَهُۥ وَلَوْ كَانُوٓاْ ءَابَآءَهُمْ أَوْ أَبْنَآءَهُمْ أَوْ إِخْوَٰنَهُمْ أَوْ عَشِيرَتَهُمْ ۚ أُوْلَـٰٓئِكَ كَتَبَ فِى قُلُوبِهِمُ ٱلْإِيمَـٰنَ وَأَيَّدَهُم بِرُوحٍ مِّنْهُ ۖ وَيُدْخِلُهُمْ جَنَّـٰتٍ تَجْرِى مِن تَحْتِهَا ٱلْأَنْهَـٰرُ خَـٰلِدِينَ فِيهَا ۚ رَضِىَ ٱللَّهُ عَنْهُمْ وَرَضُواْ عَنْهُ ۚ أُوْلَـٰٓئِكَ حِزْبُ ٱللَّهِ ۚ أَلَآ إِنَّ حِزْبَ ٱللَّهِ هُمُ ٱلْمُفْلِحُونَ ﴿٢٢﴾﴾ [المجادلة: ٢٢].

"Know, may Allāh have mercy on you, that is obligatory upon every Muslim, male and female, to learn these three matters and act according to them:

The first: That Allāh has created us, has given us sustenance, and He has not left us neglected Rather,

He has sent to us a messenger. So, whosoever obeys him will enter Paradise, and whosoever disobeys him will go to Hell.

The evidence is in His saying: "We have sent to you, (O men!) a Messenger, to be a witness concerning you, even as We sent a Messenger to Pharaoh. But Pharaoh disobeyed the Messenger; so, We seized him with a heavy Punishment." [Sūrah al-Muzzammil 73:15-16]

The second: Allāh does not pleased that anythingis associated with him in worship, not an angel close to Himor a prophet that was sent.

The evidence is in His saying: "And the places of worship are for Allāh (alone): So, invoke not any one along with Allāh." [Sūrah al-Jinn 72:18]

The third: Whoever obeys the Prophet and singles out Allāh alone in worship it is impermissible for him to take for friend those who oppose Allāh and His messenger, even if they were his nearest kin.

The evidence is in His saying: "You will not find any people who believe in Allāh and the Last Day, loving those who oppose Allāh and His Messenger, even though they were their fathers or their sons, or

their brothers, or their kindred. For such He has written Faith in their hearts, and strengthened them with a spirit from Himself. And He will admit them to Gardens beneath which Rivers flow, to dwell therein (forever). Allāh will be well pleased with them, and they with Him. They are the Party of Allāh. Truly it is the Party of Allāh that will achieve Success." [Sūrah al-Mujādilah 58:22]

Explanation

These three matters are from the most important subjects matters that are associated with Tawhīd and Allāh's rights (عَزَّوَجَلَّ).

Allāh (سُبْحَانَهُوَتَعَالَى) created the creation to worship Him. He didn't create to neglect them, in vain, or without a purpose. However, He did create them for something great, and a tremendous wisdom which contains their happiness and salvation. This is that they worship Allāh alone without any partners as Allāh (سُبْحَانَهُوَتَعَالَى) says,

﴿ وَمَا خَلَقْتُ ٱلْجِنَّ وَٱلْإِنسَ إِلَّا لِيَعْبُدُونِ ﴿٥٦﴾ ﴾

"And I (Allāh) created not the jinn's and humans except they should worship Me (Alone)." [*Sūrah Adh-Dhariyat* 51:56]

This is the worship which they were ordered with His (سُبْحَانَهُۥ وَتَعَالَىٰ) statement,

﴿ يَٰٓأَيُّهَا ٱلنَّاسُ ٱعْبُدُوا۟ رَبَّكُمُ ﴾

"O mankind! Worship your Lord (Allāh)," [*Sūrah al-Baqarah* 2:21]

He (سُبْحَانَهُۥ وَتَعَالَىٰ) says,

﴿ ۞ وَقَضَىٰ رَبُّكَ أَلَّا تَعْبُدُوٓا۟ إِلَّآ إِيَّاهُ ﴾

"And your Lord has decreed that you worship none but Him." [*Sūrah al-Israa* 17:23]

He (سُبْحَانَهُۥ وَتَعَالَىٰ) says,

﴿ ۞ وَٱعْبُدُوا۟ ٱللَّهَ وَلَا تُشْرِكُوا۟ بِهِۦ شَيْـًٔا ۖ ﴾

"Worship Allāh and join none with Him in worship." [*Sūrah an-Nisā'* 4:36]

He (سُبْحَانَهُوَتَعَالَىٰ) says,

﴿ فَٱعْبُدِ ٱللَّهَ مُخْلِصًا لَّهُ ٱلدِّينَ ۝٢ ﴾

"So, worship Allāh (Alone) by doing religious deeds sincerely for Allāh's sake only," [*Sūrah az-Zumar* 39:2]

He (سُبْحَانَهُوَتَعَالَىٰ) says,

﴿ وَمَآ أُمِرُوٓاْ إِلَّا لِيَعْبُدُواْ ٱللَّهَ مُخْلِصِينَ لَهُ ٱلدِّينَ ﴾

"And they were commanded not, but that they should worship Allāh." [*Sūrah al-Bayyinah* 98:5]

Many of these verses contains Allāh's command to worship Him alone. This worship is to single out Allāh alone (Tawhīd) and to . and specify worship for Him from supplication, fear, hope, trust in Allāh, ambition, fright, Ṣalāh, fasting, and etc.

Allāh is deserving of worship excluding everyone else besides Him. carrying out the commands and staying away from the prohibitions falls under this. So, fulfilling the commands which Allāh and His Messenger orders, abandoning the prohibitions which Allāh and His Messenger has forbidden all of this falls under worship. This is Islām, the correct religion, true faith, and guidance.

So, pray only to Allāh. bow only to than Allāh. we do not slaughter for other than Him, Do not make Du'aa to other than Allāh. Do not trust other than Allāh, and other acts of worship.

Asking for assistance from someone that is present and able to assist you then this is not worship just as Allāh (سُبْحَانَهُۥ وَتَعَالَىٰ) said in the story of Mūsā (عَلَيْهِ ٱلسَّلَامُ),

﴿ فَٱسْتَغَٰثَهُ ٱلَّذِى مِن شِيعَتِهِۦ عَلَى ٱلَّذِى مِنْ عَدُوِّهِۦ ﴾

"The man of his (own) party asked him for help against his foe," [*Sūrah al-Qasas* 28:15]

Indeed, Mūsā was able to assist him.

As for making Duʿā to a dead person or a person who is not present and cannot hear you, idols, jinn, or trees all of that is shirk, and major shirk whichAllāh (سُبْحَانَهُۥ وَتَعَالَىٰ) speaks about,

﴿ إِنَّ ٱلشِّرْكَ لَظُلْمٌ عَظِيمٌ ﴿١٣﴾ ﴾

"Joining others in worship with Allāh is a great Zulm (wrong) indeed." [*Sūrah Luqmān* 31:13]

Allāh (سُبْحَانَهُۥوَتَعَالَىٰ) says,

﴿ وَلَوْ أَشْرَكُوا۟ لَحَبِطَ عَنْهُم مَّا كَانُوا۟ يَعْمَلُونَ ﴿٨٨﴾ ﴾

"But if they had joined in worship others with Allāh, all that they used to do." [*Sūrah al-Anaam* 6:88]

He (سُبْحَانَهُۥوَتَعَالَىٰ) also says,

﴿ إِنَّ ٱللَّهَ لَا يَغْفِرُ أَن يُشْرَكَ بِهِۦ وَيَغْفِرُ مَا دُونَ ذَٰلِكَ لِمَن يَشَآءُ ۚ ﴾

"Verily! Allāh forgives not (the sin of) setting up partners in worship with Him, but He forgives whom he pleases." [*Sūrah an-Nisā'* 4:48 & 116]

He (سُبْحَانَهُۥوَتَعَالَىٰ) says,

﴿ وَلَقَدْ أُوحِيَ إِلَيْكَ وَإِلَى ٱلَّذِينَ مِن قَبْلِكَ لَئِنْ أَشْرَكْتَ لَيَحْبَطَنَّ عَمَلُكَ وَلَتَكُونَنَّ مِنَ ٱلْخَاسِرِينَ ﴿٦٥﴾ ﴾

"And indeed, it has been revealed to you (O Muḥammad ﷺ), as it was to those (Allāh's Messengers) before you: "If you join others in worship with Allāh, (then) surely (all) your deeds will be in vain, and you will certainly be among the losers." [*Sūrah az-Zumar* 39:65]

So, Allāh created us and provides for us, yet did not leave us neglected. Rather, He orders us to single Him out with Tawhīd, obey Him, and abandon acts of disobedience.

he sent us a Messenger and he is: Muḥammad(عَلَيْهِ ٱلصَّلَاةُ وَٱلسَّلَامُ). the Quran was revealed to him so we can be upright upon guidance., So, that we implement his commands and and stay away from the prohibitions, at the hands of the Muḥammad (ﷺ)the seal of the Prophets and Messenger. He came to teach mankind their religion, for he is the seal of the Prophets and their Leader and the best of them.

So, whoever obeys this Prophet and remain upright on his religion will have Paradise. Whoever disobey this Prophet and opposes his religion will have Hell. Allāh (سُبْحَانَهُۥ وَتَعَالَىٰ) says,

﴿ إِنَّآ أَرْسَلْنَآ إِلَيْكُمْ رَسُولًا شَٰهِدًا عَلَيْكُمْ ﴾

"Verily, We have sent to you (O men) a Messenger (Muḥammad صَلَّى ٱللَّهُ عَلَيْهِ وَسَلَّمَ) to be a witness over you." [*Sūrah Muzzammil* 73:15]

Meaning: a witness over your acts which he witnessed,

﴿ كَمَآ أَرْسَلْنَآ إِلَىٰ فِرْعَوْنَ رَسُولًا ۝١٥ ﴾

"As We did send a Messenger [Mūsā (Moses)] to Fir'aun (Pharaoh)." [*Sūrah Muzzammil* 73:15]

He was a Messenger (عَلَيْهِ ٱلصَّلَاةُ وَٱلسَّلَامُ),

﴿ فَعَصَىٰ فِرْعَوْنُ ٱلرَّسُولَ فَأَخَذْنَٰهُ أَخْذًا وَبِيلًا ۝١٦ ﴾

"But Fir'aun (Pharaoh) disobeyed the Messenger [Mūsā (Moses)], so We seized him with a severe punishment." [*Sūrah Muzzammil* 73:16]

Meaning: we punished him with a painful punishment in this life and punish him with Hell in the hereafter.

<u>And the second matter:</u> an actualization of the first matter which is that you know that Allāh is not pleased that anyone shares worship with Him. Just as He is the Creator, the Provider, the Giver of Death and life who created you and give you blessings. Hence, He is not pleased with anyone from the creation is associated with Him (in worship); not a sent messenger, or a close angel, and not anything else, because worship is for Allāh alone just as Allāh (سُبْحَانَهُ وَتَعَالَى) says,

﴿ ۞ وَقَضَىٰ رَبُّكَ أَلَّا تَعْبُدُوٓا۟ إِلَّآ إِيَّاهُ ﴾

"And your Lord has decreed that you worship none but Him." [*Sūrah al-Israa* 17:23]

And He (سُبْحَانَهُ وَتَعَالَى) says,

﴿ إِيَّاكَ نَعْبُدُ وَإِيَّاكَ نَسْتَعِينُ ۝٥ ﴾

"You (Alone) we worship, and You (Alone) we ask for help." [*Sūrah al-Faatihah* 1:5]

That is because associating partners with Allāh is the greatest sin which is mentioned in numerous verses. These verses order sincere worship to Allāh alone and forbid worship other than him. So, both matters should be gathered and believe that Allāh is the creator, provider, giver of life and death. So, belief that He (سُبْحَانَهُۥوَتَعَالَىٰ) is deserving of worship like slaughtering, Ṣalāh, and other acts of worship like Allāh (سُبْحَانَهُۥوَتَعَالَىٰ) says,

﴿ وَإِلَٰهُكُمْ إِلَٰهٌ وَاحِدٌ ﴾

"And your Ilah (God) is One Ilah (God - Allāh)." [*Sūrah al-Baqarah* 2:163]

He (سُبْحَانَهُۥوَتَعَالَىٰ) also says,

﴿ فَلَا تَدْعُوا۟ مَعَ ٱللَّهِ أَحَدًا ١٨ ﴾

"So, invoke not anyone along with Allāh." [*Sūrah al-Jinn* 72:18]

<u>this is the third matter:</u> which is among the most significant of obligations that every Muslim, male and female, must learn. Taking the polytheists as allies and having love for them is impermissible. It is religious duty upon whoever obeys Allāh and His Messenger and singles out Allāh (عَزَّوَجَلَّ) with Tawhīd to have enmity and hate the disbelievers for Allāh's sake. Allegiance to them and having love for them is impermissible due to the statement of Allāh (سُبْحَانَهُۥوَتَعَالَىٰ) ,

﴿ لَّا تَجِدُ قَوْمًا ﴾

"You (O Muḥammad صَلَّىٱللَّهُعَلَيْهِوَسَلَّمَ) will not find any people." [*Sūrah al-Mujādilah* 58:22]

Meaning: O Muḥammad! you will not find people of true faith and belief…

﴿ يُوَآدُّونَ مَنْ حَآدَّ ٱللَّهَ وَرَسُولَهُۥ ﴾

"making friendship with those who oppose Allāh and His Messenger (Muḥammad صَلَّىٱللَّهُعَلَيْهِوَسَلَّمَ)."[*Sūrah al-Mujādilah* 58:22]

Allāh (سُبْحَانَهُۥوَتَعَالَىٰ) says,

﴿ ۞ يَٰٓأَيُّهَا ٱلَّذِينَ ءَامَنُواْ لَا تَتَّخِذُواْ ٱلْيَهُودَ وَٱلنَّصَٰرَىٰٓ أَوْلِيَآءَ بَعْضُهُمْ أَوْلِيَآءُ بَعْضٍ وَمَن يَتَوَلَّهُم مِّنكُمْ فَإِنَّهُۥ مِنْهُمْ إِنَّ ٱللَّهَ لَا يَهْدِى ٱلْقَوْمَ ٱلظَّٰلِمِينَ ٥١ ﴾

"O you who believe! Take not the Jews and the Christians as Awliyā' (friends, protectors, helpers, etc.), they are but Awliyā' to one another. And if any amongst you takes them as Awliyā', then surely he is one of them. Verily, Allāh guides not those people who are the Zālimūn (polytheists and wrong-doers and unjust)." [*Sūrah Al-Ma'idah* 5:51]

He (عَزَّوَجَلَّ) says,

﴿ قَدْ كَانَتْ لَكُمْ أُسْوَةٌ حَسَنَةٌ فِىٓ إِبْرَٰهِيمَ وَٱلَّذِينَ مَعَهُۥٓ إِذْ قَالُواْ لِقَوْمِهِمْ إِنَّا بُرَءَٰٓؤُاْ مِنكُمْ وَمِمَّا تَعْبُدُونَ مِن دُونِ ٱللَّهِ كَفَرْنَا بِكُمْ وَبَدَا بَيْنَنَا وَبَيْنَكُمُ ٱلْعَدَٰوَةُ وَٱلْبَغْضَآءُ أَبَدًا حَتَّىٰ تُؤْمِنُواْ بِٱللَّهِ وَحْدَهُۥٓ ﴾

"Indeed, there has been an excellent example for you in Ibrāhīm (Abraham) and those with him,

> **when they said to their people: "Verily, we are free from you and whatever you worship besides Allāh, we have rejected you, and there has started between us and you, hostility and hatred for ever, until you believe in Allāh Alone,"** [*Sūrah al-Mumtahinah* 60:4]

Having dislike and enmity for the enemies of Allāh and having compassion and love for the believers is a religiously incumbent the Muslim. In the same fashion, the believer must love the Awliyā of Allāh, cooperate with them upon good, hate the enemies of Allāh, dislike them for Allāh's sake. This enmity must remain even they are called to Islām and even if they are allowed to reside in the Muslim land and they pay the *Jizyah* to the Muslim leader. This is on part that the Messenger (صَلَّى ٱللَّٰهُ عَلَيْهِ وَسَلَّمَ) took the *Jizyah* from the Jews, the Christians, and the fire worshippers. This taking of the *Jizyah* from them serves as an aid for the Muslims. It wasn't collected because of love for them. Rather, it was collected if they did not accept Islām and they were spared.

However, if they refused to accept Islām and pay the *Jizyah* they will not be spared if it is in Muslims' ability. This ruling is specific to the people of the Book and the fire worshippers. As for the rest of the disbelievers, then the *Jizyah* will not be accepted from them and they will be fought until they accept Islām like the pagans, communist, and the likes among the disbelievers. This is due to the statement of Allāh (سُبْحَانَهُ وَتَعَالَىٰ),

﴿ وَقَـٰتِلُوهُمْ حَتَّىٰ لَا تَكُونَ فِتْنَةٌ وَيَكُونَ ٱلدِّينُ كُلُّهُۥ لِلَّهِ ﴾

"And fight them until there is no more Fitnah (disbelief and polytheism: i.e. worshipping others besides Allāh) and the religion (worship) will all be for Allāh Alone." [*Sūrah al-Anfaal* 8:39**]**

He (سُبْحَانَهُ وَتَعَالَىٰ) says,

﴿ ٱنفِرُوا۟ خِفَافًا وَثِقَالًا وَجَـٰهِدُوا۟ بِأَمْوَٰلِكُمْ وَأَنفُسِكُمْ فِى سَبِيلِ ٱللَّهِ ۚ ذَٰلِكُمْ خَيْرٌ لَّكُمْ إِن كُنتُمْ تَعْلَمُونَ ۝٤١ ﴾

"March forth, whether you are light (being healthy, young and wealthy) or heavy (being ill, old and poor), strive hard with your wealth and your lives in the Cause of Allāh. This is better for you, if you but knew." [*Sūrah At-Tawbah* 9:41]

He (سُبۡحَانَهُۥ وَتَعَالَىٰ) says,

﴿ فَإِذَا ٱنسَلَخَ ٱلۡأَشۡهُرُ ٱلۡحُرُمُ فَٱقۡتُلُواْ ٱلۡمُشۡرِكِينَ حَيۡثُ وَجَدتُّمُوهُمۡ وَخُذُوهُمۡ وَٱحۡصُرُوهُمۡ وَٱقۡعُدُواْ لَهُمۡ كُلَّ مَرۡصَدٖۚ فَإِن تَابُواْ وَأَقَامُواْ ٱلصَّلَوٰةَ وَءَاتَوُاْ ٱلزَّكَوٰةَ فَخَلُّواْ سَبِيلَهُمۡۚ إِنَّ ٱللَّهَ غَفُورٞ رَّحِيمٞ ٥ ﴾

"Then when the Sacred Months (the 1st, 7th, 11th, and 12th months of the Islāmic calendar) have passed, then kill the Mushrikūn (see V.2:105) wherever you find them, and capture them and besiege them, and prepare for them each and every ambush. But if they repent and perform As-Salat (Iqamat-as-Salat), and give Zakat, then leave their way free. Verily, Allāh is Oft-Forgiving, Most Merciful." [*Sūrah At-Tawbah* 9:5]

Verses under this subject matter are abundant.

What is intended by Allāh's (سُبۡحَانَهُۥ وَتَعَالَىٰ) statement "**having the ability to do that**" is just as what is mentioned in the verse,

﴿ لَا يُكَلِّفُ ٱللَّهُ نَفْسًا إِلَّا وُسْعَهَا ﴾

"Allāh burdens not a person beyond his scope." [*Sūrah al-Baqarah* 2:286]

He (سُبْحَانَهُ وَتَعَالَىٰ) says,

﴿ فَٱتَّقُوا۟ ٱللَّهَ مَا ٱسْتَطَعْتُمْ ﴾

"So, keep your duty to Allāh and fear Him as much as you can." [*Sūrah at-Taghaabun* 64:16]

The Prophet (صَلَّىٰ ٱللَّهُ عَلَيْهِ وَسَلَّمَ) did not fight against the polytheists until he had the strength. Afterward, Allāh (سُبْحَانَهُ وَتَعَالَىٰ) says in the last part of Sūrah al-Mujādilah,

﴿ أُو۟لَـٰٓئِكَ كَتَبَ فِى قُلُوبِهِمُ ٱلْإِيمَـٰنَ وَأَيَّدَهُم بِرُوحٍ مِّنْهُ ﴾

"For such He has written Faith in their hearts, and strengthened them with *Rūh* (proofs, light and true guidance) from Himself." [Sūrah al-Mujādilah 58:22]

Meaning, gave them strength.

The author (رَحِمَهُ ٱللَّهُ) said,

اِعْلَمْ أَرْشَدَكَ اللهُ لِطَاعَتِهِ, أَنَّ الْحَنِيفِيَّةَ مِلَّةَ إِبْرَاهِيمَ أَنْ تَعْبُدَ اللهَ مُخْلِصًا لَهُ الدِّينَ. وَ بِذَلِكَ أَمَرَ اللهُ جَمِيعَ النَّاسِ, وَ خَلَقَهُمْ لَهَا كَمَا قَالَ تَعَالَى: ﴿وَمَا خَلَقْتُ ٱلْجِنَّ وَٱلْإِنسَ إِلَّا لِيَعْبُدُونِ ۝٥٦﴾ [الذاريات: ٥٦]. وَ مَعْنَى (يَعْبُدُونِ): يُوَحِّدُونِ. وَ أَعْظَمُ مَا أَمَرَ اللهُ بِهِ التَّوْحِيدُ, وَ هُوَ إِفْرَادُ اللهِ بِالْعِبَادَةِ, وَ أَعْظَمُ مَا نَهَى عَنْهُ الشِّرْكُ, وَ هُوَ دَعْوَةُ غَيْرِهِ مَعَهُ وَ الدَّلِيلُ قَوْلُهُ تَعَالَى: ﴿۞ وَٱعْبُدُوا۟ ٱللَّهَ وَلَا تُشْرِكُوا۟ بِهِۦ شَيْـًٔا﴾ [النساء: ٣٦]

"Know, may Allāh guide you to His obedience, that the Hanīfīyah is the creed of Ibrāhīm (Abraham), which is to worship Allāh alone, upon pure religious devotion. This is what Allāh has ordered all mankind with and He created them for this purpose (of worship). The evidence is in His saying,

"And I (Allāh) created not the jinns and humans except they should worship Me (Alone)." [Sūrah adh-Dhaariyaat 51:56]

To "worship Me" means to single Me (Allāh) alone in worship. The greatest thing that Allāh has ordered is Tawhīd. To make Allāh the sole object of worship. The greatest of what he forbade is Shirk, which is to call upon others with Allāh. The evidence is in His saying, "Worship Allāh and join none with Him in worship" [Sūrah an-Nisā' 4:36]

Explanation

He (رَحِمَهُ ٱللَّهُ) said,

اِعْلَمْ – أَرْشَدَكَ اللهُ لِطَاعَتِهِ

"Know, may Allāh guide you to His obedience"- he combined teaching and making Duʿā –

أَنَّ الْـحَـنِـيـفِـيَّـةَ مِـلَّـةَ إِبْـرَاهِـيـمَ أَنْ تَـعْـبُـدَ اللهَ مُـخْـلِـصًـا لَـهُ الـدِّيـنَ

"that the Ḥanafiyyah is the creed of Ibrahim: is to worship Allāh alone" This is what Allāh says regarding this matter of worship to His prophet Muḥammad,

﴿ ثُمَّ أَوْحَيْنَآ إِلَيْكَ أَنِ ٱتَّبِعْ مِلَّةَ إِبْرَٰهِيمَ حَنِيفًا ﴾

"Then, We have inspired you (O Muḥammad ﷺ saying): "Follow the religion of Ibrahim (Abraham) Hanifa (to worship none but Allāh." [*Sūrah an-Nahl* 16:123]

Ḥanafiyyah is the religion that has sincerity and loyalty to Allāh alone; and to abandon any partnership with him. the practitioner is he who is devoted to Allāh, opposes everything besides than Him, is genuine in worship to Him like Ibrāhīm and his followers. In this fashion were the other prophets and their followers,

He (رَحِمَهُ ٱللَّهُ) said,

وَ بِذَلِكَ أَمَرَ اللهُ جَمِيعَ النَّاسِ ، وَ خَلَقَهُمْ لَهَا

"This is what Allāh has ordered all mankind with and He created them for this purpose (of worship)"

Allāh orders mankind to single Him out alone (Tawhīd) and to be sincere (in worship). He created them to worship Him alone through their Ṣalāh, fasting, supplication, fear, hope, slaughtering, vows, and other kinds of worships, all of which for Allāh alone as He says,

﴿ ۞ وَقَضَىٰ رَبُّكَ أَلَّا تَعْبُدُوٓا۟ إِلَّآ إِيَّاهُ ﴾

"And your Lord has decreed that you worship none but Him." [*Sūrah al-Israa* 17:23]

He (سُبۡحَانَهُۥوَتَعَالَىٰ) says,

﴿ إِيَّاكَ نَعْبُدُ وَإِيَّاكَ نَسْتَعِينُ ۝٥ ﴾

"You (Alone) we worship, and You (Alone) we ask for help (for each and everything)." [*Sūrah al-Faatihah* 1:5]

He (سُبۡحَانَهُۥوَتَعَالَىٰ) says,

﴿ فَٱعْبُدِ ٱللَّهَ مُخْلِصًا لَّهُ ٱلدِّينَ ۝٢ ﴾

> **"So, worship Allāh (Alone) by doing religious deeds sincerely for Allāh's sake only."** [*Sūrah az-Zumar* 39:2]

He (سُبْحَانَهُ وَتَعَالَىٰ) says,

﴿ يَٰٓأَيُّهَا ٱلنَّاسُ ٱعْبُدُوا۟ رَبَّكُمُ ﴾

> **"O mankind! Worship your Lord (Allāh)."** [*Sūrah al-Baqarah* 2:21]

This worship is the reason for mankind's creation. It is the reason for the creation of both Jinn and Mankind. This worship is to single out Allāh alone, obey His commands, to keep away His prohibitions. Allāh (سُبْحَانَهُ وَتَعَالَىٰ) says,

﴿ وَمَا خَلَقْتُ ٱلْجِنَّ وَٱلْإِنسَ إِلَّا لِيَعْبُدُونِ ٥٦ ﴾

> **"And I (Allāh) created not the jinn's and humans except they should worship Me (Alone)."** [*Sūrah adh-Dhaariyaat* 51:56]

Meaning, single Me out alone in worship, make Me the sole object of worship by carrying out the commands and avoiding the prohibition.

He (رَحِمَهُ ٱللَّهُ) said,

وَ أَعْظَمُ مَا أَمَرَ اللهُ بِهِ التَّوْحِيدُ وَ هُوَ إِفْرَادُ اللهِ بِالْعِبَادَةِ

"The greatest thing that Allāh has ordered is Tawhīd. To make Allāh the sole object of worship." What is intended by worship is that it is only for alone. So, don't worship idols, prophets, angels, stones, Jinn, and so forth alongside Him (Allāh).

The author (رَحِمَهُ ٱللَّهُ) said,

وَ أَعْظَمُ مَا نَهَى عَنْهُ الشِّرْكُ وَ هُوَ دَعْوَةُ غَيْرِهِ مَعَهُ

"The greatest of what he forbade is Shirk, which is to call upon others with Allāh."

Allāh (سُبْحَانَهُ وَتَعَالَىٰ) says,

﴿ وَلَوْ أَشْرَكُوا۟ لَحَبِطَ عَنْهُم مَّا كَانُوا۟ يَعْمَلُونَ ٨٨ ﴾

> **"But if they had joined in worship others with (Allāh, all that they used to do would have been of no benefit to them."** [*Sūrah Al-An'am* 6:88]

And He (سُبْحَانَهُ وَتَعَالَىٰ) says,

﴿ وَلَقَدْ أُوحِيَ إِلَيْكَ وَإِلَى ٱلَّذِينَ مِن قَبْلِكَ لَئِنْ أَشْرَكْتَ لَيَحْبَطَنَّ عَمَلُكَ وَلَتَكُونَنَّ مِنَ ٱلْخَٰسِرِينَ ٦٥ ﴾

"And indeed, it has been revealed to you (O Muḥammad ﷺ), as it was to those (Allāh's Messengers) before you: "If you join others in worship with Allāh, (then) surely (all) your deeds will be in vain, and you will certainly be among the losers." [*Sūrah Az-Zumar* 39:65]

And in the two Saḥīḥ of al-Bukhārī and Muslim on the authority of ʿAbdullāh who reported:

أَيُّ الذَّنْبِ أَعْظَمُ قَالَ " أَنْ تَجْعَلَ لِلَّهِ نِدًّا وَهُوَ خَلَقَكَ ." قَالَ قُلْتُ ثُمَّ مَاذَا قَالَ " أَنْ تَقْتُلَ وَلَدَكَ خَشْيَةَ أَنْ يَطْعَمَ مَعَكَ ."." قَالَ قُلْتُ ثُمَّ مَاذَا قَالَ " أَنْ تَزْنِيَ بِحَلِيلَةِ جَارِكَ

"What is the worst sin?' He said: 'That you make an equal to Allāh, while it is He who created you.'" He said: "I said: 'Then what?' He said: 'That you kill your child fearing that he will eat with you.'" He

said: "I said: 'Then what?' He said: 'That you commit adultery with your neighbor's wife."

So, he (صَلَّىٱللَّهُعَلَيۡهِوَسَلَّمَ) explained that shirk is the greatest, most severe, andthe most dangerous sin.

And in another Ḥadīth he (صَلَّىٱللَّهُعَلَيۡهِوَسَلَّمَ) said,

أَلاَ أُنَبِّئُكُمْ بِأَكْبَرِ الْكَبَائِرِ ". قُلْنَا بَلَى يَا رَسُولَ اللَّهِ. قَالَ " الإِشْرَاكُ بِاللَّهِ

"Should I not inform you about the most grievous of the grave sins? We said yes O Messenger of Allāh; then he said: Associating anyone with Allāh."

this Ḥadīth is agreed on by both [Bukhari and Muslim].

So Tawhīd is: singling worship for Allāh alone, and shirk is: calling upon other than Allāh. You call upon him, fear him, have hope in Him, sacrifice for him, make vows to him, or anything else that is considered worship.

That is Major shirk- even if the person you are calling upon is a Prophet, a angel, Jinn, tree, or rock because of that Allāh (سُبۡحَانَهُۥوَتَعَالَىٰ) says,

﴿ ۞ وَٱعۡبُدُواْ ٱللَّهَ وَلَا تُشۡرِكُواْ بِهِۦ شَيۡـٔٗاۖ ﴾

"Worship Allāh and join none with Him in worship." [*Sūrah an-Nisā'* 4:36]

And by none meaning Nothing at all, and He (سُبْحَانَهُ وَتَعَالَىٰ) says,

﴿ وَمَآ أُمِرُوٓاْ إِلَّا لِيَعۡبُدُواْ ٱللَّهَ مُخۡلِصِينَ لَهُ ٱلدِّينَ ﴾

"And they were commanded not, but that they should worship Allāh, and worship none but Him Alone." [*Sūrah al-Bayyinah* 98:5]

So, the greatest thing Allāh ordered us with is to worshipp him alone, and the greatest thing which he has forbidden us from is associating anyone else with him.

That's why Allāh mentions ordering Tawhīd and forbidding shirk in numerous place throughout the Qur'ān.

A CLEAR SUMMARY OF THE THREE-FUNDAMENTAL PRINCIPLE

The author (رَحِمَهُ ٱللَّهُ) said:

فَإِذَا قِيلَ لَكَ: مَا الْأُصُولُ الثَّلَاثَةُ الَّتِي يَجِبُ عَلَى الْإِنْسَانِ مَعْرِفَتُهَا؟ فَقُلْ: مَعْرِفَةُ الْعَبْدِ رَبَّهُ, وَ دِينَهُ, وَنَبِيَّهُ مُحَمَّدًا – صَلَّى اللهُ عَلَيْهِ وَ سَلَّمَ.

فَإِذَا قِيلَ لَكَ: مَنْ رَبُّكَ؟ فَقُلْ: رَبِّي اللهُ الَّذِي رَبَّانِي وَ رَبَّى جَمِيعَ الْعَالَمِينَ بِنِعَمِهِ. وَ هُوَ مَعْبُودِي لَيْسَ لِي مَعْبُودٌ سِوَاهُ. وَالدَّلِيلُ قَوْلُهُ تَعَالَى: ﴿

ﵟٱلۡحَمۡدُ لِلَّهِ رَبِّ ٱلۡعَٰلَمِينَ ٢ﵞ [الفاتحة: ٢] وَ كُلُّ مَا سِوَى اللهِ عَالَمٌ وَ أَنَا وَاحِدٌ مِنْ ذَلِكَ الْعَالَمِ

"If you were asked, "What are the three fundamentals that must be understood by every Muslim?", say: " The servant should know his Rabb (Cherisher and Sustainer), his religion, and his Prophet, Muḥammad (ﷺ).

If you are asked: "Who is your Rabb (Cherisher and Sustainer)?" say: "My Rabb (Cherisher and Sustainer) is Allāh. He has nourished me and all other creatures with his blessings. He is my Deity, and I have no other besides Him." The evidence is in His saying, "Praise be to Allāh, the Cherisher and Sustainer of the worlds;" [Sūrah al-Fatihah 1:2], Everything other than Allāh is of His Creation; and I am part of that Creation."

Explanation

These three fundamental principles which gather all of the religion: "who is your Rabb, who is your prophet, what is your religion?" are matters which the servant will be asked about in his grave.

So, if someone asked, "who is your Rabb?" You say: my Rabb is the one who sustained me and all of the creation with his blessings and he is my Lord and I have no other. This is the Lord of all (that exists) just like what Allāh (سُبْحَانَهُۥ وَتَعَالَىٰ) says,

﴿ ٱلۡحَمۡدُ لِلَّهِ رَبِّ ٱلۡعَٰلَمِينَ ۝٢ ﴾

> **"All the praises and thanks be to Allāh, the Lord of the ʿĀlamīn (mankind, jinns and all that exists)."** [*Sūrah al-Faatihah* 1:2]

the word ʿĀlamīn refers to all of creation. Jinn, humans, animals, mountains, and tress. All of them are created beings. Allāh (سُبْحَانَهُۥ وَتَعَالَىٰ) says,

﴿ إِنَّ رَبَّكُمُ ٱللَّهُ ٱلَّذِى خَلَقَ ٱلسَّمَٰوَٰتِ وَٱلْأَرْضَ فِى سِتَّةِ أَيَّامٍ ثُمَّ ٱسْتَوَىٰ عَلَى ٱلْعَرْشِ يُغْشِى ٱلَّيْلَ ٱلنَّهَارَ يَطْلُبُهُۥ حَثِيثًا وَٱلشَّمْسَ وَٱلْقَمَرَ وَٱلنُّجُومَ مُسَخَّرَٰتٍۭ بِأَمْرِهِۦٓ ۗ أَلَا لَهُ ٱلْخَلْقُ وَٱلْأَمْرُ ۗ تَبَارَكَ ٱللَّهُ رَبُّ ٱلْعَٰلَمِينَ ﴿٥٤﴾ ﴾

"Indeed, your Lord is Allāh, Who created the heavens and the earth in Six Days, and then He Istawa (rose over) the Throne (really in a manner that suits His Majesty). He brings the night as a cover over the day, seeking it rapidly, and (He created) the sun, the moon, the stars subjected to His Command. Surely, His is the Creation and Commandment. Blessed be Allāh, the Lord of the 'Ālamīn (mankind, jinn's and all that exists)!" [*Sūrah al-'Arāf* 7:54]

He is the Rabb of everyone. To Allāh belongs the creation and commands. He is deserving to be worshiped. Based upon this Allāh (سُبْحَانَهُ وَتَعَالَىٰ) says,

﴿ يَٰٓأَيُّهَا ٱلنَّاسُ ٱعْبُدُوا۟ رَبَّكُمُ ﴾

"O mankind! Worship your Lord (Allāh)." [*Sūrah al-Baqarah* 2:21]

So, He is my Deity and I have no other beside Him. The proof of that is Allāh's (سُبْحَانَهُۥ وَتَعَالَىٰ) statement,

﴿ ٱلْحَمْدُ لِلَّهِ رَبِّ ٱلْعَٰلَمِينَ ۝٢ ﴾

"All the praises and thanks be to Allāh, the Lord of the ʿĀlamīn (mankind, jinns and all that exists)." [*Sūrah al-Faatihah* 1:2]

Meaning all praises belongs to Allāh and worship is a form of praise.

Everything besides Allāh is from the creation. The Jinn, mankind, animals, and mountains are all created beings , and I am one of those creations that Allāh created, brought us into existence, and made it obligatory upon his creation to obey Him. So, obeying Allāh and His Messenger and singling out Allāh alone in worship is a religious duty placed upon all of those who have been obliged, from the Jinn and Mankind, to fulfill.

In the same fashion the angels have been duty bound to worship Allāh alone. Based upon this Allāh (سُبْحَانَهُۥوَتَعَالَىٰ) says about the angels,

﴿ لَّا يَعْصُونَ ٱللَّهَ مَآ أَمَرَهُمْ وَيَفْعَلُونَ مَا يُؤْمَرُونَ ۝٦ ﴾

"Who disobey not, (from executing) the Commands they receive from Allāh, but do that which they are commanded." [*Sūrah At-Tahrīm* 66:6]

He (سُبْحَانَهُۥوَتَعَالَىٰ) also says,

﴿ لَا يَسْبِقُونَهُۥ بِٱلْقَوْلِ وَهُم بِأَمْرِهِۦ يَعْمَلُونَ ۝٢٧ يَعْلَمُ مَا بَيْنَ أَيْدِيهِمْ وَمَا خَلْفَهُمْ وَلَا يَشْفَعُونَ إِلَّا لِمَنِ ٱرْتَضَىٰ وَهُم مِّنْ خَشْيَتِهِۦ مُشْفِقُونَ ۝٢٨ ﴾

"They speak not until He has spoken, and they act on His Command. He knows what is before them, and what is behind them, and they cannot intercede except for him with whom He is pleased. And they stand in awe for fear of Him." [*Sūrah Al-Anbiyā* 21:28]

The author (رَحِمَهُ ٱللَّهُ) continues:

فَـإِذَا قِـيـلَ لَـكَ : بِـمَـا عَـرَفْـتَ رَبَّـكَ ؟ فَـقُـلْ : بِآيَـاتِـهِ وَ مَـخْـلُـوقَـاتِـهِ. وَ مِـنْ آيَـاتِـهِ اللَّـيْـلُ وَ الـنَّـهَـارُ وَ الـشَّـمْـسُ وَالْـقَـمَـرُ. وَمِـنْ مَـخْـلُـوقَـاتِـهِ : الـسَّـمَـوَاتُ الـسَّـبْـعُ , وَ الْأَرَضُـونَ الـسَّـبْـعُ وَ مَـا فِـيـهِـنَّ , وَ مَـا بَـيْـنَـهُـمَـا, وَ الـدَّلِـيـلُ قَـوْلُـهُ تَـعَـالَـى : ﴿وَمِنْ ءَايَـٰتِهِ ٱلَّيْلُ وَٱلنَّهَارُ وَٱلشَّمْسُ وَٱلْقَمَرُ ۚ لَا تَسْجُدُوا۟ لِلشَّمْسِ وَلَا لِلْقَمَرِ وَٱسْجُدُوا۟ لِلَّهِ ٱلَّذِى خَلَقَهُنَّ إِن كُنتُمْ إِيَّاهُ تَعْبُدُونَ ﴿٣٧﴾﴾ [فصلت: ٣٧] وَ الـدَّلِـيـلُ قَـوْلُـهُ تَـعَـالَـى :﴿إِنَّ رَبَّكُمُ ٱللَّهُ ٱلَّذِى خَلَقَ ٱلسَّمَـٰوَٰتِ وَٱلْأَرْضَ فِى سِتَّةِ أَيَّامٍ ثُمَّ ٱسْتَوَىٰ عَلَى ٱلْعَرْشِ يُغْشِى ٱلَّيْلَ ٱلنَّهَارَ يَطْلُبُهُۥ حَثِيثًا وَٱلشَّمْسَ وَٱلْقَمَرَ وَٱلنُّجُومَ مُسَخَّرَٰتٍۭ بِأَمْرِهِۦٓ ۗ أَلَا لَهُ ٱلْخَلْقُ وَٱلْأَمْرُ ۗ تَبَارَكَ ٱللَّهُ رَبُّ ٱلْعَـٰلَمِينَ ﴿٥٤﴾﴾ [الأعراف: ٥٤] وَ الـرَّبُّ هُـوَ الْـمَـعْـبُـودُ, وَ الـدَّلِـيـلُ قَـوْلُـهُ : ﴿يَـٰٓأَيُّهَا ٱلنَّاسُ ٱعْبُدُوا۟ رَبَّكُمُ ٱلَّذِى خَلَقَكُمْ وَٱلَّذِينَ مِن قَبْلِكُمْ لَعَلَّكُمْ تَتَّقُونَ

﴿٢١﴾ ٱلَّذِى جَعَلَ لَكُمُ ٱلْأَرْضَ فِرَٰشًا وَٱلسَّمَآءَ بِنَآءً وَأَنزَلَ مِنَ ٱلسَّمَآءِ مَآءً فَأَخْرَجَ بِهِۦ مِنَ ٱلثَّمَرَٰتِ رِزْقًا لَّكُمْ ۖ فَلَا تَجْعَلُوا۟ لِلَّهِ أَندَادًا وَأَنتُمْ تَعْلَمُونَ ﴿٢٢﴾ ﴾ [البقرة: ٢١ – ٢٢]. قَالَ ابْنُ كَثِيرٍ: الْخَالِقُ لِهَذِهِ الْأَشْيَاءِ هُوَ الْمُسْتَحِقُّ لِلْعِبَادَةِ

"If you were asked: "How did you know your Rabb (Cherisher and Sustainer)?" say: "Through His signs and His creatures. Among his signs are the Night, Day, the Sun, and the Moon. Among His creation are the Heavens, the Earth, and all that is in and between them." The evidence is in His saying: "Among His Signs are the Night and the Day, and the Sun and the Moon. Prostrate not to the Sun and the Moon, but prostrate to Allāh, Who created them, if it is Him you wish to serve." [Sūrah Fussilāt 41:37]

And His saying: "Your Guardian Rabb (Cherisher and Sustainer) is Allāh, Who created the heavens and the earth in six days, then He settled Himself on the Throne: He draws the Night as a veil o'er the Day, each seeking the other in rapid succession: and the Sun, the Moon, and the stars, (all) are subservient by His Command. Verily, His are the Creation and the Command. Blessed be Allāh, the

Cherisher and Sustainer of the Worlds! "[Sūrah al-ʿArāf 7:54]

The "the word Rabb here refers to the worshipped Deity. The evidence to this is in His saying: "O you people! Worship your Guardian Rabb (Cherisher and Sustainer), who created you and those who came before you, that you may become righteous; Who has made the earth your couch, and the heavens your canopy; and sent down rain from the heavens; and brought forth therewith Fruits for your sustenance; then set not up rivals unto Allāh when you know (the truth)." [Sūrah al-Baqarah 2:21-22]

Ibn Kathīr (رَحِمَهُ ٱللَّهُ) said, "The creator of all these things is the only one deserving to be worshiped."

Explanation

He said (رَحِمَهُ ٱللَّهُ),

إِذَا قِيلَ لَكَ

"if you were asked" O Muslim! how do you come know your lord that you worship? Say: I come to know Him by His signs and His creation., Meaning, I come to learn about Allāh by His numerous signs and His tremendous creations that demonstrates that He is the Magnificent Lord, The Creator and All-Knowing, and He is the only one who deserves worship. Thus, He is the one who creates whatever He wants, gives, prevents, benefits, and harms (as He wills). Everything is in His Hands (سُبْحَانَهُ وَتَعَالَىٰ).

So, Allāh is the only one deserving of our worship by giving obedience to Him, supplicating to Him, seeking relief from agony, as well as the rest of our deeds and acts of worship. All of this because Allāh had created us for this purpose. Allāh (سُبْحَانَهُ وَتَعَالَىٰ) says,

﴿ وَمَا خَلَقْتُ ٱلْجِنَّ وَٱلْإِنسَ إِلَّا لِيَعْبُدُونِ ﴿٥٦﴾ ﴾

"And I (Allāh) created not the jinns and humans except they should worship Me (Alone)." [*Sūrah Adh-Dhariyat* 51:56]

This worship as mentioned in the previous verse is the Tawhīd, obedience, adherence to His legislation, giving tremendous importance to His commands and prohibition in speech as well as action.

The proof of learning about Allāh by way His signs is in Allāh's (سُبْحَانَهُ وَتَعَالَىٰ) statement,

﴿ وَمِنْ ءَايَـٰتِهِ ٱلَّيْلُ وَٱلنَّهَارُ وَٱلشَّمْسُ وَٱلْقَمَرُ ﴾

"And from among His Signs are the night and the day, and the sun and the moon." [*Sūrah Fussilāt* 41:37]

All of this demonstrates that Allāh is The Lord of all that exists and that He is The Creator, All-Knowing. He brings the night through it darkness, and brings the day through its sunlight. Afterward, he causes the day to arrive and the night to depart.

The Sun rises over the entire world and mankind benefit by it. The same for the moon at night. There are other tremendous signs like the earth and what's it contains of mountains, rivers, seas, trees, and animals. The heavens which people see all of which are signs that demonstrate His Majesty, that He is the Lord of all that exists, the Creator, All-Knowing, and the One deserving of worship. So, based upon this Allāh says,

﴿ وَمِنْ ءَايَٰتِهِ ٱلَّيْلُ وَٱلنَّهَارُ وَٱلشَّمْسُ وَٱلْقَمَرُ ۚ لَا تَسْجُدُوا۟ لِلشَّمْسِ وَلَا لِلْقَمَرِ وَٱسْجُدُوا۟ لِلَّهِ ٱلَّذِى خَلَقَهُنَّ إِن كُنتُمْ إِيَّاهُ تَعْبُدُونَ ﴿٣٧﴾ ﴾

"And from among His Signs are the night and the day, and the sun and the moon. Prostrate not to the sun nor to the moon, but prostrate to Allah Who created them, if you (really) worship Him." [*Sūrah Fussilāt* 41:37]

Meaning: do not worship these created things; rather worship the One who created and brought them into existence. The servant shows humility, submission, obedience (to Allāh's commands), and abstaining (from His prohibitions) because He is the only one deserving of it. All of this is done with veneration, reverence, fear, and hope for the reward (with Allāh).

Allāh (سُبْحَانَهُ وَتَعَالَىٰ) says,

﴿ إِنَّ رَبَّكُمُ ٱللَّهُ ﴾

"Verily, your Lord is Allāh" [*Sūrah al-'Arāf* 7:54]

Meaning, O servants from the Jinn and mankind! Your Lord is Allāh. Your Lord is your Creator and one true deity who has no partners,

﴿ ٱلَّذِى خَلَقَ ٱلسَّمَٰوَٰتِ وَٱلْأَرْضَ فِى سِتَّةِ أَيَّامٍ ثُمَّ ٱسْتَوَىٰ عَلَى ٱلْعَرْشِ ﴾

"Indeed, your Lord is Allāh, Who created the heavens and the earth in Six Days, and then He Istawā (rose over) the Throne (really in a manner that suits His Majesty." [*Sūrah al-'Arāf* 7:54]

Meaning, He rose and ascended above the Throne.

So, His knowledge encompasses every places. Yet, He is above his throne, above all of His creation. His throne which is the ceiling of the creation is the uppermost of creation and Allāh is above everything. then He ascended above it (the Throne) in a manner befitting of Majesty. none of His attributes resembles the creation. Allāh (سُبْحَانَهُ وَتَعَالَىٰ) says,

﴿ لَيْسَ كَمِثْلِهِۦ شَىْءٌ ۖ وَهُوَ ٱلسَّمِيعُ ٱلْبَصِيرُ ١١ ﴾

"There is nothing like unto Him, and He is the All-Hearer, the All-Seer." [*Sūrah ash-Shūrā* 42:11]

He (سُبْحَانَهُ وَتَعَالَىٰ) says,

﴿ وَلَمْ يَكُن لَّهُۥ كُفُوًا أَحَدٌۢ ٤ ﴾

"And there is none co-equal or comparable unto Him." [*Sūrah al-Ikhlās* 112:4]

The author (رَحِمَهُ ٱللَّهُ) then mentioned the statement of Allāh (سُبْحَانَهُ وَتَعَالَىٰ),

﴿ يُغْشِى ٱلَّيْلَ ٱلنَّهَارَ يَطْلُبُهُۥ حَثِيثًا ﴾

"He brings the night as a cover over the day, seeking it rapidly." [*Sūrah al-'Arāf* 7:54]

Meaning: they

envelop one another.

﴿ يَطْلُبُهُۥ حَثِيثًا ﴾

"seeking it rapidly"

Meaning: it seeks one another fast. When one finishes the other enters. This will happen in this manner until .

﴿ وَٱلشَّمۡسَ وَٱلۡقَمَرَ ﴾

"the sun, the moon"

Allāh created the sun, moon, and stars. He has made them subjugated, obedient, and submissive to His commands.

Then He (سُبۡحَانَهُۥوَتَعَالَىٰ) says,

﴿ أَلَا لَهُ ٱلۡخَلۡقُ وَٱلۡأَمۡرُۗ ﴾

"Surely, His is the Creation and Commandment."

The creation and command both belong to Allāh. He is the Supreme Creator that his universal command is undeniable and carried on the people just as Allāh (سُبۡحَانَهُۥوَتَعَالَىٰ) says,

﴿ إِنَّمَآ أَمۡرُهُۥٓ إِذَآ أَرَادَ شَيۡـًٔا أَن يَقُولَ لَهُۥ كُن فَيَكُونُ ٨٢ ﴾

"Verily, His Command, when He intends a thing, is only that He says to it, "Be!" and it is!" [*Sūrah Ya-Sin* 36:82]

He (سُبۡحَانَهُۥ وَتَعَالَىٰ) says,

﴿ وَمَآ أَمۡرُنَآ إِلَّا وَٰحِدَةٞ كَلَمۡحِۭ بِٱلۡبَصَرِ ٥٠ ﴾

"And Our Commandment is but one, as the twinkling of an eye." [*Sūrah al-Qamar* 54:50]

So, Allāh's universal, ordained commands are unpreventable and based upon this Allāh says,

﴿ أَلَا لَهُ ٱلۡخَلۡقُ وَٱلۡأَمۡرُۗ تَبَارَكَ ٱللَّهُ رَبُّ ٱلۡعَٰلَمِينَ ٥٤ ﴾

"His is the Creation and Commandment. Blessed be Allāh, the Lord of the ʿĀlamīn (mankind, jinns and all that exists)!" [*Sūrah al-ʿArāf* 7:54]

Tabārak (Blessed): the highest degree of blessing in which this wording is only used for Allāh. So, you cannot say to a servant "Tabārak so-and-so person" this is specific to Allāh just as He (سُبۡحَانَهُۥ وَتَعَالَىٰ) says,

﴿ تَبَٰرَكَ ٱلَّذِى بِيَدِهِ ٱلْمُلْكُ ﴾

"Blessed is He in Whose Hand is the dominion, and He is Able to do all things." [*Sūrah al-Mulk* 67:1]

You can say to something from the creation, "*Bārak Allāh* [5]so-and-so" or, "so-and-so *Mubārak*" or, "*Tabārakta*[6]"" but 'Tabārak' is only for Allāh alone.

وَ الرَّبُّ

"And 'Rabb'" is the one true deity. ('Ālamīn) are all of the creation from the jinn, mankind, the sky, and the earth. He (سُبْحَانَهُ وَتَعَالَىٰ) is its Lord. The Lord and Creator (جَلَّ وَعَلَا) of everything.

Allāh (سُبْحَانَهُ وَتَعَالَىٰ) says,

﴿ يَٰٓأَيُّهَا ٱلنَّاسُ ٱعْبُدُوا۟ رَبَّكُمُ ٱلَّذِى خَلَقَكُمْ وَٱلَّذِينَ مِن قَبْلِكُمْ لَعَلَّكُمْ تَتَّقُونَ ٢١ ﴾

[5] **TN:** this phrase is a supplication asking for blessing.
[6] **TN:** this is the past tense form of تبارك

"O mankind! Worship your Lord (Allāh), Who created you and those who were before you so that you may become Al-Muttaqûn (the pious - see V.2:2)." [*Sūrah al-Baqarah* 2:21]

He created everything that came before us, came after us (from the time of Ādam, before him and after him. Allāh created everything for the purpose of being religious and worship Him alone just as Allāh says (سُبْحَانَهُ وَتَعَالَى),

﴿ لَعَلَّكُمْ تَتَّقُونَ ﴿٢١﴾ ﴾

"so that you may become Al-Muttaqûn (the pious)." [*Sūrah al-Baqarah* 2:21]

Then Allāh explained some of his actions in which He (سُبْحَانَهُ وَتَعَالَى) says,

﴿ ٱلَّذِى جَعَلَ لَكُمُ ٱلْأَرْضَ فِرَٰشًا وَٱلسَّمَآءَ بِنَآءً ﴾

"who has made the earth a resting place for you" [*Sūrah al-Baqarah* 2:22]

He made the earth a place of rest for mankind. He made it a flat land for mankind to build upon, live on, sleep on, and walk upon. He also anchored mountains on it.

Then He (سُبْحَانَهُ وَتَعَالَىٰ) says,

﴿ وَٱلسَّمَآءَ بِنَآءً ﴾

"and the sky as a canopy,"

Allāh built the sky as a canopy and a protective roof; yet they are in denial of his signs. He also adorned it with stars, the sun, and the moon.

﴿ وَأَنزَلَ مِنَ ٱلسَّمَآءِ مَآءً ﴾

"and sent down water from the sky" from the clouds.

﴿ فَأَخْرَجَ بِهِۦ مِنَ ٱلثَّمَرَٰتِ رِزْقًا لَّكُمْ ﴾

"and brought forth therewith fruits as a provision for you" diverse types of provision in every place. Allāh brings the earth to life after it was dead.

Then He (سُبْحَانَهُ وَتَعَالَىٰ) says,

﴿ فَلَا تَجْعَلُوا۟ لِلَّهِ أَندَادًا وَأَنتُمْ تَعْلَمُونَ ٢٢ ﴾

"Then do not set up rivals unto Allāh (in worship) while you know." [*Sūrah al-Baqarah* 2:22]

Meaning, don't set up things that falsely resemble or made to be parallel in which you worship alongside Allāh. Not any idols, Jinn, angels, and so forth..

So, worship is a right that belongs to Allāh alone. He doesn't have any rival, equal, or match in this . Rather, He is the one true deity . the Mushrikūn used to take rivals from idols, Jinn, and angels in which they worship and seek relief (from hardship) beside Allāh. So, Allāh rejected this action from them. Allāh made it clear that the creation is undeserving and have no right to worship. Nor does the creation possess any power to do anything without Allāh (سُبۡحَانَهُۥوَتَعَالَىٰ) having given prior permission and decree.

Al-Ḥāfiẓ Ibn Kathīr (رَحِمَهُ ٱللَّهُ) said in his Tafsīr of the verse,

The creator of these things from heavens, earth, fruits, trees, rain, and so forth. He (سُبۡحَانَهُۥوَتَعَالَىٰ) is deserving to be worshiped and obeyed because He is the Lord, Master, and Creator of all thing just as Allāh (سُبۡحَانَهُۥوَتَعَالَىٰ) says,

﴿ وَإِلَٰهُكُمْ إِلَٰهٌ وَاحِدٌ ۖ لَّا إِلَٰهَ إِلَّا هُوَ الرَّحْمَٰنُ الرَّحِيمُ ﴿١٦٣﴾ ﴾

"And your Ilāh (God) is One Ilāh (God - Allāh), Lā ilāha illa Huwa (there is none who has the right to be worshipped but He), the Most Beneficent, the Most Merciful." [*Sūrah al-Baqarah* 2:163]

MEANING OF WORSHIP AND TYPES

The author (رَحِمَهُ ٱللَّهُ) said:

. وَأَنْوَاعُ الْعِبَادَةِ الَّتِي أَمَرَ اللهُ بِهَا مِثْلَ الْإِسْلَامِ وَ الْإِيمَانِ وَ الْإِحْسَانِ, وَ مِنْهُ الدُّعَاءُ , وَ الْخَوْف, وَ الرَّجَاءُ, وَ التَّوَكُّلُ, وَ الرَّغْبَةُ , وَالرَّهْبَةُ, وَ الْخُشُوعُ , وَالْخَشْيَةُ , وَالْإِنَابَةُ, وَالْإِسْتِعَانَةُ, وَالْإِسْتِعَاذَةُ , وَ الْإِسْتِغَاثَةُ, وَالذَّبْحُ, وَالنَّذْرُ, وَ غَيْرُ ذَلِكَ مِنْ أَنْوَاعِ الْعِبَادَةِ الَّتِي أَمَرَ اللهُ بِهَا , كُلُّهَا للهِ تَعَالَى. وَ الدَّلِيلُ قَوْلُهُ تَعَالَى : ﴿ وَأَنَّ ٱلْمَسَٰجِدَ لِلَّهِ فَلَا تَدْعُواْ مَعَ ٱللَّهِ أَحَدًا ﴿١٨﴾ ﴾ [الجن: ١٨]. فَمَنْ صَرَفَ مِنْهَا شَيْئًا لِغَيْرِ اللهِ , فَهُوَ مُشْرِكٌ كَافِرٌ وَ الدَّلِيلُ قَوْلُهُ تَعَالَى: ﴿ وَمَن

يَدْعُ مَعَ ٱللَّهِ إِلَـٰهًا ءَاخَرَ لَا بُرْهَـٰنَ لَهُۥ بِهِۦ فَإِنَّمَا حِسَابُهُۥ عِندَ رَبِّهِۦٓ ۚ إِنَّهُۥ لَا يُفْلِحُ ٱلْكَـٰفِرُونَ ﴿١١٧﴾ ﴾ [المؤمنون: ١١٧]. وَ فِي الْحَدِيثِ : ((الدُّعَاءُ مُخُّ الْعِبَادَةِ)). وَ الدَّلِيلُ : قَوْلُهُ تَعَالَى : ﴿ وَقَالَ رَبُّكُمُ ٱدْعُونِىٓ أَسْتَجِبْ لَكُمْ ۚ إِنَّ ٱلَّذِينَ يَسْتَكْبِرُونَ عَنْ عِبَادَتِى سَيَدْخُلُونَ جَهَنَّمَ دَاخِرِينَ ﴿٦٠﴾ ﴾ [غافر: ٦٠].

"There are various forms of worship which Allāh commanded like Islām, ʾĪmān, and ʾIḥsān. So, from that is Duʿā (supplication), Khawf (fear), Rajāʾ (hope), Tawakkul (trust), Raghbah (aspiration), Raḥbah (dread), Khushūʿ (submissiveness), Khashiyah (knowledge-based fear), ʾInābah (turn repentantly to Allāh), ʾIstiʿānah (seeking assistance), ʾIstiʿādhah (seeking refuge), ʾIstighāthah (to seek succor), Dhabḥ (sacrifice), Nadhar (vowing), and other forms of worship which Allāh (سُبْحَانَهُۥوَتَعَالَىٰ) commanded. All of which is a right belonging to Allāh alone .

The evidence to that is His (سُبْحَانَهُۥوَتَعَالَىٰ) saying,

"And the places of worship are for Allāh (alone): So, invoke not any one along with Allāh." [Sūrah al-Jinn 72:18]

So, whoever directs any part of it (worship) to other than Allāh then he is a polytheist and an disbeliever. The evidence to this is His saying, "If anyone invokes, besides Allāh, any other god, he has no authority therefore; and his reckoning will be only with his Rabb (Cherisher and Sustainer)! And verily the Disbelievers shall not prosper!" [Sūrah al-Mu'minīn 23:117]

It was narrated in the Ḥadīth: "supplication is the essence of worship." and the evidence is in His (سُبْحَانَهُ وَتَعَالَىٰ) saying:

"And your Rabb (Cherisher and Sustainer) says: 'Call on Me; I will answer your (prayer): but those who are too arrogant to serve Me will surely enter Hell abased!'" [Sūrah Ghāfir 40:60]

<u>Explanation</u>

Worship has diverse types. Among them is Islām and its pillars. So, everything Allāh ordered from the actions of Islām is considered worship. From Ṣalāh, fasting, and so forth. The same can be said with ʾĪmān and its inner actions; like believing in Allāh, his angels, his books, his messengers, the last day, and the good and bad of the divine decree. and The same can be said for fear, love, and hope etc.

So, everything that has something to do with heart falls under worship. The same for ʾIḥsān, **"that you worship Allāh as if you can see him"** this also is from worship. It (ʾIḥsān) is the highest and greatest form of worship.

It is obligatory on every responsible person to have sincere devotion in their worship of Allāh alone. Thus, do not worship prophets, righteous people, idols, trees, rocks, or stars alongside Allāh. Because worship is a right that belongs to Allāh alone. He (سُبْحَانَهُ وَتَعَالَىٰ) says,

﴿ وَأَنَّ ٱلْمَسَٰجِدَ لِلَّهِ فَلَا تَدْعُوا۟ مَعَ ٱللَّهِ أَحَدًا ﴿١٨﴾ ﴾

"And the mosques are for Allāh (Alone), so invoke not anyone along with Allāh." [*Sūrah al-Jinn* 72:18]

He (سُبْحَانَهُۥوَتَعَالَىٰ) says,

﴿ إِيَّاكَ نَعۡبُدُ وَإِيَّاكَ نَسۡتَعِينُ ۝٥ ﴾

"You (Alone) we worship, and You (Alone) we ask for help (for each and everything)." [*Sūrah al-Fātihah* 1:5]

He (سُبْحَانَهُۥوَتَعَالَىٰ) also says,

﴿ وَلَا تَدۡعُ مِن دُونِ ٱللَّهِ مَا لَا يَنفَعُكَ وَلَا يَضُرُّكَۖ فَإِن فَعَلۡتَ فَإِنَّكَ إِذٗا مِّنَ ٱلظَّٰلِمِينَ ۝١٠٦ ﴾

"And invoke not besides Allāh, any that will neither profit you, nor hurt you, but if (in case) you did so, you shall certainly be one of the Zâlimûn (polytheists and wrong-doers)." [*Sūrah Yūnus* 10:106]

He (سُبْحَانَهُۥوَتَعَالَىٰ) said,

﴿ وَمَن يَدْعُ مَعَ ٱللَّهِ إِلَٰهًا ءَاخَرَ لَا بُرْهَٰنَ لَهُۥ بِهِۦ فَإِنَّمَا حِسَابُهُۥ عِندَ رَبِّهِۦٓۚ إِنَّهُۥ لَا يُفْلِحُ ٱلْكَٰفِرُونَ ﴿١١٧﴾ ﴾

"And whoever invokes (or worships), besides Allāh, any other ilāh (god), of whom he has no proof, then his reckoning is only with his Lord. Surely! Al-Kāfirūn (the disbelievers in Allāh and in the Oneness of Allāh, polytheists, pagans, idolaters, etc.) will not be successful." [*Sūrah al-Mu'minun* 23:117]

Also, He (سُبْحَانَهُۥ وَتَعَالَىٰ) says,

﴿ يُولِجُ ٱلَّيْلَ فِي ٱلنَّهَارِ وَيُولِجُ ٱلنَّهَارَ فِي ٱلَّيْلِ وَسَخَّرَ ٱلشَّمْسَ وَٱلْقَمَرَ كُلٌّ يَجْرِي لِأَجَلٍ مُّسَمًّىۚ ذَٰلِكُمُ ٱللَّهُ رَبُّكُمْ لَهُ ٱلْمُلْكُۚ وَٱلَّذِينَ تَدْعُونَ مِن دُونِهِۦ مَا يَمْلِكُونَ مِن قِطْمِيرٍ ﴿١٣﴾ إِن تَدْعُوهُمْ لَا يَسْمَعُوا۟ دُعَآءَكُمْ وَلَوْ سَمِعُوا۟ مَا ٱسْتَجَابُوا۟ لَكُمْۖ وَيَوْمَ ٱلْقِيَٰمَةِ يَكْفُرُونَ بِشِرْكِكُمْۚ وَلَا يُنَبِّئُكَ مِثْلُ خَبِيرٍ ﴿١٤﴾ ﴾

"He merges the night into the day (i.e. the decrease in the hours of the night are added to the hours of the day), and He merges the day into the night (i.e. the decrease in the hours of the day are added to the hours of the night). And He has subjected the sun and the moon, each runs its course for a term appointed. Such is Allāh your Lord; His is the kingdom. And those, whom you invoke or call upon instead of Him, own not even a Qitmīr -the thin membrane over the date-stone- If you invoke (or call upon) them, they hear not your call, and if (in case) they were to hear, they could not grant it (your request) to you. And on the Day of Resurrection, they will disown your worshipping them. And none can inform you (O Muḥammad صَلَّىٱللَّهُعَلَيْهِوَسَلَّمَ) like Him Who is the All Knower (of each and everything)." [*Sūrah Fātir* 35:13-14]

So Allāh (سُبْحَانَهُوَتَعَالَىٰ) called their supplication Shirk. So, being sincerely devoted to Allāh alone in worship is a religious duty upon all those held accountable. That sincere devotion is to be in their Rajā', fear, 'Isti'ānah, 'Istighāthah, slaughtering, vows, Khashiyah of Allāh, Ṣalāh, fasting, and so forth. All these diverse acts of worship belong to Allāh alone.

So, anyone who tries to attain nearness to Allāh through supplicating to a Wali, a prophet, an idol, a tree, or a stone; or by slaughtering, vows, Ṣalāh, fasting, or similar to that then he polytheist and disbeliever. He has also worshiped that beside Allāh just like the polytheists in the beginning. Those individuals who worshiped graves, trees, stones, and idols. Based upon this Allāh (عَزَّوَجَلَّ) says,

﴿ وَلَوْ أَشْرَكُوا۟ لَحَبِطَ عَنْهُم مَّا كَانُوا۟ يَعْمَلُونَ ﴿٨٨﴾ ﴾

"But if they had joined in worship others with Allāh, all that they used to do would have been of no benefit to them." [*Sūrah Al-ʾAnʿām* 6:88]

He (سُبْحَانَهُۥوَتَعَالَىٰ) says,

﴿ إِنَّهُۥ مَن يُشْرِكْ بِٱللَّهِ فَقَدْ حَرَّمَ ٱللَّهُ عَلَيْهِ ٱلْجَنَّةَ وَمَأْوَىٰهُ ٱلنَّارُ ﴾

"Verily, whosoever sets up partners in worship with Allāh, then Allāh has forbidden Paradise for him, and the Fire will be his abode. And for the Zâlimûn (polytheists and wrong-doers) there are no helpers." [*Sūrah Al-Māʾidah* 5:72]

Also, He (سُبۡحَانَهُۥ وَتَعَالَىٰ) says,

﴿ وَلَقَدْ أُوحِىَ إِلَيْكَ وَإِلَى ٱلَّذِينَ مِن قَبْلِكَ لَئِنْ
أَشْرَكْتَ لَيَحْبَطَنَّ عَمَلُكَ وَلَتَكُونَنَّ مِنَ ٱلْخَٰسِرِينَ
٦٥ بَلِ ٱللَّهَ فَٱعْبُدْ وَكُن مِّنَ ٱلشَّٰكِرِينَ ٦٦ ﴾

> **"And indeed, it has been revealed to you (O Muḥammad صَلَّى ٱللَّهُ عَلَيْهِ وَسَلَّمَ), as it was to those (Allāh's Messengers) before you: "If you join others in worship with Allāh, (then) surely (all) your deeds will be in vain, and you will certainly be among the losers - Nay! But worship Allāh (Alone and none else), and be among the grateful." [Sūrah az-Zumar 39:65-66]**

It is a religious duty of have sincere devotion to Allāh alone in all of these forms of worship. So, whoever directs any of that to another than Allāh whether it is an idol, stone, tree, or a grave, is a polytheist and a disbeliever based upon Allāh's (سُبۡحَانَهُۥ وَتَعَالَىٰ) statement,

﴿ وَمَن يَدْعُ مَعَ ٱللَّهِ إِلَٰهًا ءَاخَرَ لَا بُرْهَٰنَ لَهُۥ بِهِۦ فَإِنَّمَا حِسَابُهُۥ عِندَ رَبِّهِۦٓ إِنَّهُۥ لَا يُفْلِحُ ٱلْكَٰفِرُونَ ﴿١١٧﴾ ﴾

"And whoever invokes (or worships), besides Allāh, any other ilāh (god), of whom he has no proof, then his reckoning is only with his Lord. Surely! Al-Kāfirūn (the disbelievers in Allāh and in the Oneness of Allāh, polytheists, pagans, idolaters, etc.) will not be successful." [*Sūrah al-Mu'minun* 23:117]

There are other previous verses illustrate this and is a proof of what was mentioned prior.

In the Ḥadīth,

الدُّعَاءُ مُخُّ الْعِبَادَةِ

"supplication is the essence of worship"

Allāh (سُبْحَانَهُ وَتَعَالَىٰ) says,

﴿ وَقَالَ رَبُّكُمُ ٱدْعُونِىٓ أَسْتَجِبْ لَكُمْ ۚ إِنَّ ٱلَّذِينَ يَسْتَكْبِرُونَ عَنْ عِبَادَتِى سَيَدْخُلُونَ جَهَنَّمَ دَاخِرِينَ ﴿٦٠﴾ ﴾

> **"And your Lord said: "Invoke Me, [i.e. believe in My Oneness (Islâmic Monotheism)] (and ask Me for anything) I will respond to your (invocation). Verily! Those who scorn My worship [i.e. do not invoke Me, and do not believe in My Oneness, (Islâmic Monotheism)] they will surely enter Hell in humiliation!"** [*Sūrah Ghāfir* 40:60]

So, Allāh called Duʿā (invocation) worship in His statement, **"Verily! Those who scorn My worship"** meaning scorn supplicating to Me.

The author (رَحِمَهُ ٱللَّهُ) then said,

فَالدُّعَاءُ

"**So Duʿā**" is to appeal to Allāh by supplicating to Him, asking for salvation and provision; all of which is worship. So if one was to direct that to an idol, tree, stone, or the dead he would become one who ascribes partners to Allāh (عَزَّوَجَلَّ). So, it is obligatory to be on guard from Shirk and all of its subtly and significant aspects; and that worship is for Allāh alone. but appealing to a living capable person for something that he can do is not a problem and is not considered Shirk.

So, if you asked your brother who present, O ʿAbdullāh! help me cut down this tree, or dig a well, that is no problem just as Allāh (سُبْحَانَهُۥ وَتَعَالَىٰ) says in the story of Mūsā,

﴿ فَٱسْتَغَٰثَهُ ٱلَّذِى مِن شِيعَتِهِۦ عَلَى ٱلَّذِى مِنْ عَدُوِّهِۦ ﴾

"The man of his (own) party asked him for help against his foe." [*Sūrah al-Qasas* 28:15]

So, the Israeli asked for help from Mūsā against the Copt. Because Mūsā was capable to recuse him; he (Mūsā) was also among the speaking and hearing (the living).

But if you depend on one of the creation for something that only Allāh can do; it doesn't matter if that person is presence, absent, or dead and he believes that one whom he is supplicating to can cause bring benefit or cause him harm, not by means related to physical senses, then this a form of major Shirk just as Allāh related what the polytheists said,

﴿ هَٰٓؤُلَآءِ شُفَعَٰٓؤُنَا عِندَ ٱللَّهِ ﴾

"These are our intercessors with Allāh." [*Sūrah Yūnus* 10:18]

They thought that by worshiping them that they can intercede before Allāh to help them get what they want, or help them get closer to Allāh.

Just like what Allāh (سُبْحَانَهُ وَتَعَالَىٰ) mentioned about them in this verse,

﴿ مَا نَعْبُدُهُمْ إِلَّا لِيُقَرِّبُونَآ إِلَى ٱللَّهِ زُلْفَىٰٓ ﴾

"We worship them only that they may bring us near to Allāh." [*Sūrah az-Zumar* 39:3]

This happened on part of their ignorance and misguidance concerning the one giving and receiving intercession.

All intercession belongs to Allāh. Allāh administers the affairs of His servant as He pleases. Hence, intercession is only granted to the one whom Allāh is pleased with their deeds; and no one is allowed to seek intercession with Allāh except after permission is grant by Him just as Allāh (سُبْحَانَهُ وَتَعَالَىٰ) says,

﴿ مَن ذَا ٱلَّذِى يَشْفَعُ عِندَهُۥٓ إِلَّا بِإِذْنِهِۦ ﴾

"Who is he that can intercede with Him except with His Permission?" [*Sūrah al-Baqarah* 2:255]

He (سُبْحَانَهُ وَتَعَالَىٰ) also says,

﴿ وَلَا يَشْفَعُونَ إِلَّا لِمَنِ ٱرْتَضَىٰ ﴾

"and they cannot intercede except for him with whom He is pleased." [*Sūrah al-Anbiyā* 21:28]

So, intercession can only be granted after receiving Allāh's permission and He is content with the one seeking it. Allāh is only pleased with t the people of Tawhīd as the Prophet (صَلَّى ٱللَّهُ عَلَيْهِ وَسَلَّمَ) said. Abū Hurayrah (رَضِيَ ٱللَّهُ عَنْهُ) asked,

يَا رَسُولَ اللَّهِ، مَنْ أَسْعَدُ النَّاسِ بِشَفَاعَتِكَ يَوْمَ الْقِيَامَةِ قَالَ رَسُولُ اللَّهِ صلى الله عليه وسلم " لَقَدْ ظَنَنْتُ يَا أَبَا هُرَيْرَةَ أَنْ لاَ يَسْأَلَنِي عَنْ هَذَا الْحَدِيثِ أَحَدٌ أَوَّلُ مِنْكَ، لِمَا رَأَيْتُ مِنْ حِرْصِكَ عَلَى الْحَدِيثِ، أَسْعَدُ النَّاسِ بِشَفَاعَتِي يَوْمَ الْقِيَامَةِ مَنْ قَالَ لاَ إِلَهَ إِلاَّ اللَّهُ، خَالِصًا مِنْ قَلْبِهِ

"O Allah's Messenger (صَلَّى ٱللَّهُ عَلَيْهِ وَسَلَّمَ)! Who will be the happiest person, who will gain your intercession on the Day of Resurrection?" Allāh's Messenger (صَلَّى ٱللَّهُ عَلَيْهِ وَسَلَّمَ) said: O Abu Huraira! " I have thought that none will ask me about it before you as I know

> **your longing for the (learning of) Hadiths. The happiest person who will have my intercession on the Day of Resurrection will be the one who said sincerely from the bottom of his heart "None has the right to be worshipped but Allāh."[7]**

Therefore, intercession will only be given to the people of Tawhīd and ʾĪmān whom Allāh is pleased with their statements and actions.

[7] Collected by al-Bukhārī his Ṣaḥīḥ No. (99) and No. (6570).

MENTIONING SOME OF THE ACTS OF WORSHIP

The author (رَحِمَهُ ٱللَّهُ) said,

. وَ دَلِيلُ الْخَوْفِ قَوْلُهُ تَعَالَى: ﴿فَلَا تَخَافُوهُمْ وَخَافُونِ إِن
كُنتُم مُّؤْمِنِينَ ﴿١٧٥﴾﴾ [آل عمران: ١٧٥]. وَ دَلِيلُ الرَّجَاءِ قَوْلُهُ
تَعَالَى: ﴿فَمَن كَانَ يَرْجُواْ لِقَآءَ رَبِّهِۦ فَلْيَعْمَلْ عَمَلًا صَٰلِحًا وَلَا يُشْرِكْ بِعِبَادَةِ رَبِّهِۦٓ
أَحَدًۢا ﴿١١٠﴾﴾ [الكهف: ١١٠]. وَ دَلِيلُ التَّوَكُّلِ قَوْلُهُ تَعَالَى:
﴿وَعَلَى ٱللَّهِ فَتَوَكَّلُوٓاْ إِن كُنتُم مُّؤْمِنِينَ ﴿٢٣﴾﴾ [المائدة: ٢٣]. وَ قَوْلُهُ
تَعَالَى: ﴿وَمَن يَتَوَكَّلْ عَلَى ٱللَّهِ فَهُوَ حَسْبُهُۥٓ﴾ [الطلاق: ٣]. وَ دَلِيلُ
الرَّغْبَةِ وَ الرَّهْبَةِ وَالْخُشُوعِ قَوْلُهُ تَعَالَى: ﴿إِنَّهُمْ

كَانُوا۟ يُسَٰرِعُونَ فِى ٱلْخَيْرَٰتِ وَيَدْعُونَنَا رَغَبًا وَرَهَبًا ۖ وَكَانُوا۟ لَنَا خَٰشِعِينَ ﴿٩٠﴾ ﴾ [الأنبياء: ٩٠]. وَ دَلِيلُ الْخَشْيَةِ قَوْلُهُ تَعَالَى : ﴿ فَلَا تَخْشَوْهُمْ وَٱخْشَوْنِى ﴾ [البقرة: ١٥٠] . وَ دَلِيلُ الْإِنَابَةِ قَوْلُهُ : ﴿ وَأَنِيبُوٓا۟ إِلَىٰ رَبِّكُمْ وَأَسْلِمُوا۟ لَهُۥ ﴾ [الزمر: ٥٤]. وَ دَلِيلُ الْإِسْتِعَانَةِ قَوْلُهُ تَعَالَى : ﴿ إِيَّاكَ نَعْبُدُ وَإِيَّاكَ نَسْتَعِينُ ﴿٥﴾ ﴾ [الفاتحة: ٥] . وَ فِي الْحَدِيثِ : ((إِذَا اسْتَعَنْتَ فَاسْتَعِنْ بِاللهِ)) وَ دَلِيلُ الْإِسْتِعَاذَةِ قَوْلُهُ تَعَالَى : ﴿ قُلْ أَعُوذُ بِرَبِّ ٱلْفَلَقِ ﴿١﴾ ﴾ [الفلق: ١]. وَ قَوْلُهُ تَعَالَى : ﴿ قُلْ أَعُوذُ بِرَبِّ ٱلنَّاسِ ﴿١﴾ ﴾ [الناس: ١]. وَ دَلِيلُ الْإِسْتِغَاثَةِ قَوْلُهُ تَعَالَى : ﴿ إِذْ تَسْتَغِيثُونَ رَبَّكُمْ فَٱسْتَجَابَ لَكُمْ ﴾ [الأنفال: ٩]. وَ دَلِيلُ الذَّبْحِ قَوْلُهُ تَعَالَى : ﴿ قُلْ إِنَّ صَلَاتِى وَنُسُكِى وَمَحْيَاىَ وَمَمَاتِى لِلَّهِ رَبِّ ٱلْعَٰلَمِينَ ﴿١٦٢﴾ لَا شَرِيكَ لَهُۥ ۖ وَبِذَٰلِكَ أُمِرْتُ وَأَنَا۠ أَوَّلُ ٱلْمُسْلِمِينَ ﴿١٦٣﴾ ﴾ [الأنعام: ١٦٢ – ١٦٣]. وَ مِنَ السُّنَّةِ : ((لَعَنَ اللهُ مَنْ ذَبَحَ لِغَيْرِ اللهِ)) وَ دَلِيلُ النَّذْرِ قَوْلُهُ

تَـعَـالَـى : ﴿ يُوفُونَ بِٱلنَّذْرِ وَيَخَافُونَ يَوْمًا كَانَ شَرُّهُۥ مُسْتَطِيرًا ۝٧ ﴾ [الإنسان: ٧].

And the Evidence to Khawf (fearing) Allāh alone is in His (سُبْحَانَهُ وَتَعَالَىٰ) saying, "Be you not afraid of them, but fear Me, if you have faith." [Sūrah ʾĀli ʿImrān 3:175]

Evidence of Rajāʾ (hope) is in His (سُبْحَانَهُ وَتَعَالَىٰ) saying, "Whoever expects to meet his Rabb (Cherisher and Sustainer), let him work righteousness, and, in the worship of his Rabb (Cherisher and Sustainer), admit no one as partner." [Sūrah al-Kahf 18:110]

Evidence of Tawakkul (trust) is in His (سُبْحَانَهُ وَتَعَالَىٰ) saying, "But on Allāh put your trust if you have faith." [Sūrah al-Māʾidah 5:23] and His saying, "And if any one puts his trust in Allāh, sufficient is (Allāh) for him." [Sūrah at-Ṭalāq 65:3]

Evidence of Raghbah (aspiration), Raḥbah (dread), Khushūʿ (submissiveness) is in His (سُبْحَانَهُ وَتَعَالَىٰ) saying, "They used to call on Us with yearning and awe, and humble themselves before Us." [Sūrah al-Anbiyā 21:90]

Evidence of Khashiyah (knowledge-based fear) is in His (سُبۡحَانَهُۥ وَتَعَالَىٰ) saying, "So fear them not, but fear Me; and that I may complete My favors on you, and you may (consent to) be guided." [Sūrah al-Baqarah 2:150]

Evidence of 'Inābah (turn repentantly to Allāh) is in His (سُبۡحَانَهُۥ وَتَعَالَىٰ) saying, "Turn you to your Rabb (Cherisher and Sustainer) (in repentance) and submit to Him, before the chastisement comes on you: after that you shall not be helped." [Sūrah az-Zumar 39:54]

Evidence of 'Istiʿānah (seeking assistance) is in His (سُبۡحَانَهُۥ وَتَعَالَىٰ) saying, "You Alone do we worship, and Your aid we seek." [Sūrah al-Fātihah 1:5] and from the Ḥadīth, "If you seek aid, supplication to Allāh for aid."

Evidence of 'Istiʿādhah (seeking refuge) is in His (سُبۡحَانَهُۥ وَتَعَالَىٰ) saying, "Say: I seek refuge with the Rabb (Cherisher and Sustainer) and Cherisher of Mankind, The King of Mankind." [Sūrah al-Ikhlās 114:1-2]

Evidence of 'Istighāthah (to seek succor) is in His (سُبۡحَانَهُۥ وَتَعَالَىٰ) saying, "Remember you implored the

assistance of your Rabb (Cherisher and Sustainer), and He answered you: 'I will assist you with a thousand of the angels, ranks on ranks.'" [Sūrah al-Anfāl 8:9]

Evidence of Dhabḥ (sacrifice) is in His (سُبۡحَانَهُۥ وَتَعَالَىٰ) saying, "Say: 'Truly, my prayer and my service of sacrifice, my life and my death, are (all) for Allāh, the Cherisher of the Worlds: No partner hath He: this am I commanded, and I am the first of those who submit to His will.'" [Sūrah al-ʾAnʿām 6:162] And from the Hadīth, "Allāh's curse is upon those who offer sacrifices to other then Him."

Evidence of Nadhar (vowing) is in His (سُبۡحَانَهُۥ وَتَعَالَىٰ) saying: "They perform (their) vows, and they fear a Day whose evil flies far and wide." [Sūrah al-Insān 76:7]

Explanation

The author (رَحِمَهُ ٱللَّهُ) mentioned some types of worship, among them is Khawf (fear) which has three categories::

__**The First:**__ Secret Fear which is exclusively for Allāh. Because He is capable of all things and He should be feared as Allāh (سُبْحَانَهُ وَتَعَالَىٰ) says,

﴿ فَلَا تَخَافُوهُمْ وَخَافُونِ إِن كُنتُم مُّؤْمِنِينَ ﴿١٧٥﴾ ﴾

"So, fear them not, but fear Me, if you are (true) believers." [*Sūrah ʾĀli ʿImrān* 3:175]

He (سُبْحَانَهُ وَتَعَالَىٰ) says,

﴿ وَلَمْ يَخْشَ إِلَّا ٱللَّهَ ﴾

"and fear none but Allāh." [*Sūrah at-Tawbah* 9:18]

He (سُبْحَانَهُ وَتَعَالَىٰ) also says,

﴿ فَلَا تَخْشَوُا۟ ٱلنَّاسَ وَٱخْشَوْنِ ﴾

"Therefore, fear not men but fear Me." [*Sūrah al-Māʾidah* 5:44]

So, having Khashiyah (knowledge-based fear) and Khawf (fear) of Allāh is mandatory. Because He is capable of turning the hearts and has power over all things; capable of bringing benefit, harm, giving, and taking away. Making this type of fear exclusive for Allāh is obligatory and only Allāh should be feared at this level in all cases.

One normally has this level of fear because of an exclusive ability that which is not perceived by what one senses. This is the reason why the grave worshippers believe that some people have the power to administer things in the creation along with Allāh (جَلَّ وَعَلَا). They also believe that as it pertains to idols, Jinn, and so forth; and this is major Shirk. In addition, they believe that those things possess the ability to give, prevent, deviate the hearts, and cause death without any natural causes.

<u>The second:</u> fear caused by what one senses: just like what Allāh mentioned in the story of ʾUḥud when it was told to the Prophet (صَلَّى ٱللَّٰهُ عَلَيْهِ وَسَلَّمَ) that the Polytheist have gathered together and turned against you. So, Allāh revealed about this matter,

﴿ إِنَّمَا ذَٰلِكُمُ ٱلشَّيْطَٰنُ يُخَوِّفُ أَوْلِيَآءَهُۥ فَلَا تَخَافُوهُمْ وَخَافُونِ إِن كُنتُم مُّؤْمِنِينَ ١٧٥ ﴾

"It is only Shayṭān (Satan) that suggests to you the fear of his Awliyā [supporters and friends (polytheists, disbelievers in the Oneness of Allāh and in His Messenger, Muḥammad (صَلَّى ٱللَّهُ عَلَيْهِ وَسَلَّمَ)], so fear them not, but fear Me, if you are (true) believers." [*Sūrah ʾĀli ʿImrān* 3:175]

So Shayṭān scares people with his supporters, and make them seem big in their hearts so they can fear them, and Allāh (سُبْحَانَهُ وَتَعَالَىٰ) says, **"so fear them not"** yet depend on Me, and prepare yourselves and do not care about them as Allāh (سُبْحَانَهُ وَتَعَالَىٰ) says in another verse,

﴿ وَأَعِدُّوا۟ لَهُم مَّا ٱسْتَطَعْتُم مِّن قُوَّةٍ ﴾

"And make ready against them all you can of power." [*Sūrah al-ʾAnfāl* 8:60]

This is fear caused by what one senses and its ok. However, the secret fear, fear from the heart, that is what is forbidden.

But fear caused by what one senses like fearing a thief, a burglar, or an enemy one should prepare the necessary weapons. This matter is obligatory due to what Allāh (سُبْحَانَهُ وَتَعَالَىٰ) says,

﴿ يَـٰٓأَيُّهَا ٱلَّذِينَ ءَامَنُوا۟ خُذُوا۟ حِذْرَكُمْ ﴾

"O you who believe! Take your precautions." [*Sūrah an-Nisā'* 4:71]

Allāh says about Mūsā when he left Egypt afraid of Pharaoh and his people,

﴿ فَخَرَجَ مِنْهَا خَآئِفًا يَتَرَقَّبُ ﴾

"So, he escaped from there, looking about in a state of fear." [*Sūrah al-Qasas* 28:21]

This is fear caused by what one senses and its ok. But fearing the enemy should not keep you from making Jihād, aiding and supporting the truth.This type of fear should only carry one to prepare before facing the enemy and taking precaution.

The third: natural fear: is apart the natural disposition of man. This type of fear is not blameworthy. For example, one being afraid of a snake, scorpion, or predatory animal. So, in this case he should distance himself from it and kill it; or he should distance himself from their habitat so he won't get harmed.

This matter is unavoidable as Allāh placed this natural disposition within us to protect us from harm. For instance, we fear the cold and as a result we wear heavy clothes. We fear hunger and as a result we eat. We fear thirst so as a result we drink. All of these things are natural.

In the same manner for Rajā᾿ (hope) it is a form of worship which is exclusive to Allāh. So, we have hope in Allāh. and have good thoughts of Allāh just He (سُبْحَانَهُ وَتَعَالَىٰ) says,

﴿ فَمَن كَانَ يَرْجُوا۟ لِقَآءَ رَبِّهِۦ فَلْيَعْمَلْ عَمَلًا صَٰلِحًا وَلَا يُشْرِكْ بِعِبَادَةِ رَبِّهِۦٓ أَحَدًۢا ﴿١١٠﴾ ﴾

"So, whoever hopes for the Meeting with his Lord, let him work righteousness and associate none as a partner in the worship of his Lord." [*Sūrah Al-Kahf* 18:110]

So, Raghbah (aspiration) for Allāh and Rajā᾿ (hoping) for His reward is all acts of worship to Him. Allāh (سُبْحَانَهُ وَتَعَالَىٰ) says,

﴿ إِنَّهُمْ كَانُوا۟ يُسَٰرِعُونَ فِى ٱلْخَيْرَٰتِ وَيَدْعُونَنَا رَغَبًا وَرَهَبًا ۖ وَكَانُوا۟ لَنَا خَٰشِعِينَ ﴿٩٠﴾ ﴾

"Verily, they used to hasten on to do good deeds, and they used to call on Us with hope and fear, and used to humble themselves before Us." [*Sūrah Al-Anbiyā* 21:90]

So, Raghbah (aspiration) is Rajā' (hope) and Raḥbah (awe) is Khawf (fear). Both are forms of worship in which the servant is obliged to think good of his Lord and act according to the legislated guidelines. Indeed, having good thoughts (of Allāh) coupled with the legislated means comes back to the servant in the form of good, mercy, entering Jannah, and forgiveness of sins.

The same for Tawakkul (trust) is also a form of worship which one entrusts Allāh, depends completely on Him along with taking by the necessary means. So, you depend on Allāh for protection from evil and temptation, obtaining provision, entering Jannah, deliverance from Hell along with taking the legislated means. Allāh (سُبْحَانَهُ وَتَعَالَىٰ) says,

﴿ وَعَلَى ٱللَّهِ فَتَوَكَّلُوٓاْ إِن كُنتُم مُّؤۡمِنِينَ ٢٣ ﴾

"and put your trust in Allāh if you are believers indeed." [*Sūrah al-Mā'idah* 5:23]

He (سُبْحَانَهُ وَتَعَالَىٰ) also says,

﴿ وَمَن يَتَوَكَّلْ عَلَى ٱللَّهِ فَهُوَ حَسْبُهُۥٓ ﴾

"And whosoever puts his trust in Allāh, then He will suffice him." [*Sūrah at-Ṭalāq* 65:3]

Meaning, the Tawakkul in Allāh is appropriate for him.

The same for Raghbah (aspiration), Raḥbah (awe), and Khashiyah (knowledge-based fear) of Allāh. All of these are forms of worship. Allāh (سُبْحَانَهُ وَتَعَالَىٰ) says about the Prophets and the righteous,

﴿ إِنَّهُمْ كَانُوا۟ يُسَٰرِعُونَ فِى ٱلْخَيْرَٰتِ وَيَدْعُونَنَا رَغَبًا وَرَهَبًا ۖ وَكَانُوا۟ لَنَا خَٰشِعِينَ ﴿٩٠﴾ ﴾

"Verily, they used to hasten on to do good deeds, and they used to call on Us with hope and fear, and used to humble themselves before Us." [*Sūrah al-Anbiyā* 21:90]

They were afraid of Allāh, humble to Him.

'Inābah (turn repentantly to Allāh) is a form of worship in which Allāh (سُبْحَانَهُ وَتَعَالَىٰ) says,

﴿ وَأَنِيبُوٓاْ إِلَىٰ رَبِّكُمۡ وَأَسۡلِمُواْ لَهُۥ ﴾

"And turn in repentance and in obedience with true Faith to your Lord and submit to Him." [*Sūrah az-Zumar* 39:54]

ʾInābah (turn repentantly to Allāh) means to return to Allāh, penitence to Him, and to maintain the correct path to His obedience. This is a form of worship to Allāh which is a duty upon everyone to turn in repentance to Allāh, return to the Truth, and stay on the path of his obedience.

ʾIstiʿānah (seeking assistance) is a form of worship just as Allāh (سُبۡحَانَهُۥوَتَعَالَىٰ) says,

﴿ إِيَّاكَ نَعۡبُدُ وَإِيَّاكَ نَسۡتَعِينُ ۝٥ ﴾

"You (Alone) we worship, and You (Alone) we ask for help (for each and everything)." [*Sūrah al-Fatihah* 1:5]

And in the Ḥadīth,

إِذَا اسْتَعَنْتَ فَاسْتَعِنْ بِاللهِ

"and when you seek assistance, seek Allāh's aid."

So, the servant should seek assistance from Allāh. For instance, you would say, "O Allāh aid me in remembering you and thanking you" "O Allāh aid me in obeying you", "O Allāh aid me in everything good" etc.. So, you should seek aid from Allāh in all important matters.

Also, ʾIstiʿādhah (seeking refuge) is worship in which you seek refuge with Allāh from all evil and resort to Him just like what Allāh (سُبۡحَانَهُۥوَتَعَالَىٰ) says,

﴿ قُلۡ أَعُوذُ بِرَبِّ ٱلۡفَلَقِ ۝١ ﴾

> **"Say, "I seek refuge with (Allāh) the Lord of the daybreak."** [*Sūrah al-Falaq* 113:1]

He (سُبۡحَانَهُۥوَتَعَالَىٰ) also says,

﴿ قُلۡ أَعُوذُ بِرَبِّ ٱلنَّاسِ ۝١ ﴾

> **"Say, "I seek refuge with (Allāh) the Lord of mankind."** [*Sūrah an-Nās* 114:1]

Seeking refuge with Allāh from the Shayṭān, everything harmful, and every enemy is a matter duty bound just as Allāh (سُبۡحَانَهُۥوَتَعَالَىٰ) says,

﴿ وَإِمَّا يَنزَغَنَّكَ مِنَ ٱلشَّيۡطَٰنِ نَزۡغٌ فَٱسۡتَعِذۡ بِٱللَّهِۚ ﴾

"And if an evil whisper comes to you from Shayṭān (Satan) then seek refuge with Allāh. Verily, He is All-Hearer, All-Knower." [*Sūrah al-ʿArāf* 7:200]

ʾIstighāthah (to seek succor) is worship in which you ask Allāh for support intense situations that might come from an enemy, for blessed rain to come down, or for a bane to be removed just as Allāh (سُبۡحَانَهُۥوَتَعَالَىٰ) says,

﴿ إِذۡ تَسۡتَغِيثُونَ رَبَّكُمۡ فَٱسۡتَجَابَ لَكُمۡ ﴾

"when you sought help of your Lord and He answered you." [*Sūrah ʾAnfāl* 8:9]

Dhabḥ (sacrifice) is worship. Allāh (سُبۡحَانَهُۥوَتَعَالَىٰ) says,

﴿ قُلۡ إِنَّ صَلَاتِي وَنُسُكِي ﴾

"Say (O Muḥammad صَلَّىٱللَّهُعَلَيۡهِوَسَلَّمَ): "Verily, my Salat (prayer), my sacrifice"

Meaning my slaughter.

﴿ وَمَحۡيَايَ وَمَمَاتِي لِلَّهِ رَبِّ ٱلۡعَٰلَمِينَ ١٦٢ ﴾

"and my living, and my dying are for Allāh, the Lord of the 'Alamin (mankind, jinns and all that exists)." [*Sūrah al-ʾAnʿām* 6:162]

Nadhar (vowing) is worship. Allāh (سُبۡحَانَهُۥوَتَعَالَىٰ) says,

﴿ يُوفُونَ بِٱلنَّذۡرِ ﴾

"They fulfill (their) vow)." [*Sūrah Insān* 76:7]

He (سُبۡحَانَهُۥوَتَعَالَىٰ) also says,

﴿ وَمَآ أَنفَقۡتُم مِّن نَّفَقَةٍ أَوۡ نَذَرۡتُم مِّن نَّذۡرٖ فَإِنَّ ٱللَّهَ يَعۡلَمُهُۥۗ ﴾

"And whatever you spend for spending's (e.g., in Sadaqah - charity, etc. for Allāh's Cause) or whatever vow you make, be sure Allāh knows it all." [*Sūrah Al-Baqarah* 2:270]

The Prophet (صَلَّىٱللَّهُعَلَيۡهِوَسَلَّمَ) said,

مَنْ نَذَرَ أَنْ يُطِيعَ اللهَ ، فَلْيُطِعْهُ ، وَمَنْ نَذَرَ أَنْ يَعْصِيَهُ ، فَلَا يَعْصِهِ

"Whoever vows that he will be obedient to Allāh, should remain obedient to Him; and whoever made a vow that he will disobey Allāh, should not disobey Him."

So, vowing is a form of worship and an act of obedience to Allāh. When one does this act of worship he is committed to fulfilling it. Vowing is disliked because what it contains of commitment and hardship. Based upon that the Prophet (صَلَّى ٱللَّهُ عَلَيْهِ وَسَلَّمَ) forbad it.

He said,

إِنَّ النَّذْرَ لَا يَأْتِي بِخَيْرٍ

"It does not (necessarily) bring good."

However, if one took a vow to obey then he has to commit it due to the Prophet (صَلَّى ٱللَّهُ عَلَيْهِ وَسَلَّمَ) statement,

مَنْ نَذَرَ أَنْ يُطِيعَ اللهَ ، فَلْيُطِعْهُ

"whoever vowed to obey he shall do so."

So, if he vowed an act of worship like Ṣalāh, fasting, charity, or other than that he has to commit to fulfill it as previously mentioned.

THE SECOND FUNDAMENTAL PRINCIPLE: KNOWING THE RELIGION OF ISLĀM WITH PROOF

The author (رَحِمَهُ ٱللَّهُ) said,

اَلْأَصْلُ الثَّانِي : مَعْرِفَةُ دِينِ الْإِسْلَامِ بِالْأَدِلَّةِ . هُوَ الْاِسْتِسْلَامُ لِله بِالتَّوْحِيدِ ,وَالْاِنْقِيَادُ لَهُ بِالطَّاعَةِ . وَ الْبَرَاءَةُ مِنَ الشِّرْكِ وَ أَهْلِهِ . وَ هُوَ ثَلَاثُ مَرَاتِبَ : الْإِسْلَامُ , وَ الْإِيمَانُ , وَ الْإِحْسَانُ , وَ كُلُّ مَرْتَبَةٍ لَهَا أَرْكَانٌ . فَأَرْكَانُ الْإِسْلَامِ خَمْسَةٌ : شَهَادَةُ أَنْ لَا إِلَهَ إِلَّا اللهُ , وَ أَنَّ مُحَمَّدًا رَسُولُ اللهِ (صَلَّى اللهُ عَلَيْهِ وَ سَلَّمَ), وَ إِقَامُ الصَّلَاةِ وَ إِيْتَاءُ الزَّكَاةِ , وَ صَوْمُ رَمَضَانَ , وَ

حَجُّ بَيْتِ اللهِ الْحَرَامِ. فَدَلِيلُ الشَّهَادَةِ قَوْلُه ﴿ شَهِدَ
ٱللَّهُ أَنَّهُۥ لَآ إِلَٰهَ إِلَّا هُوَ وَٱلْمَلَٰٓئِكَةُ وَأُوْلُواْ ٱلْعِلْمِ قَآئِمَۢا بِٱلْقِسْطِۚ لَآ إِلَٰهَ إِلَّا هُوَ
ٱلْعَزِيزُ ٱلْحَكِيمُ ﴿١٨﴾ ﴾ وَمَعْنَاهَا: لَا مَعْبُودَ بِحَقٍّ إِلَّا اللهُ
, (لَا إِلَهَ) نَافِياً جَمِيعَ مَا يُعْبَدُ مِنْ دُونِ اللهِ. (إِلَّا
اللهُ) مُثْبِتاً الْعِبَادَةَ للهِ وَحْدَهُ لَا شَرِيكَ لَهُ فِي
عِبَادَتِهِ كَمَا لَا شَرِيكَ لَهُ فِي مُلْكِهِ. وَ تَفْسِيرُهَا
الَّذِي يُوَضِّحُهَا, قَوْلُهُ تَعَالَى: ﴿ وَإِذْ قَالَ إِبْرَٰهِيمُ لِأَبِيهِ
وَقَوْمِهِۦٓ إِنَّنِى بَرَآءٌ مِّمَّا تَعْبُدُونَ ﴿٢٦﴾ إِلَّا ٱلَّذِى فَطَرَنِى فَإِنَّهُۥ سَيَهْدِينِ ﴿٢٧﴾
وَجَعَلَهَا كَلِمَةًۢ بَاقِيَةً فِى عَقِبِهِۦ لَعَلَّهُمْ يَرْجِعُونَ ﴿٢٨﴾ ﴾ وَ قَوْلُهُ: ﴿ قُلْ
يَٰٓأَهْلَ ٱلْكِتَٰبِ تَعَالَوْاْ إِلَىٰ كَلِمَةٍ سَوَآءٍۭ بَيْنَنَا وَبَيْنَكُمْ أَلَّا نَعْبُدَ إِلَّا ٱللَّهَ وَلَا
نُشْرِكَ بِهِۦ شَيْـًٔا وَلَا يَتَّخِذَ بَعْضُنَا بَعْضًا أَرْبَابًا مِّن دُونِ ٱللَّهِۚ فَإِن تَوَلَّوْاْ
فَقُولُواْ ٱشْهَدُواْ بِأَنَّا مُسْلِمُونَ ﴿٦٤﴾ ﴾ وَ دَلِيلُ الشَّهَادَةِ أَنَّ
مُحَمَّداً رَسُولُ اللهِ (صَلَّى اللهُ عَلَيْهِ وَ سَلَّمَ), قَوْلُهُ
تَعَالَى: ﴿ لَقَدْ جَآءَكُمْ رَسُولٌ مِّنْ أَنفُسِكُمْ عَزِيزٌ عَلَيْهِ مَا
عَنِتُّمْ حَرِيصٌ عَلَيْكُم بِٱلْمُؤْمِنِينَ رَءُوفٌ رَّحِيمٌ ﴿١٢٨﴾ ﴾ وَ

مَـعْـنَـى شَـهَـادَةِ أَنَّ مُـحَـمَّـداً رَسُـولُ اللهِ (صَـلَّـى اللهُ عَـلَـيْـهِ وَ سَـلَّـمَ) : طَـاعَـتُـهُ فِـيـمَـا أَمَـرَ, وَ تَـصْـدِيـقُـهُ فِـيـمَـا أَخْـبَـرَ وَاجْـتِـنَـابُ مَـا نَـهَـى عَـنْـهُ وَ زَجَـرَ, وَ أَنَّ لَا يُـعْـبَـدُ اللهُ إِلَّا بِـمَـا شَـرَعَ. وَ دَلِـيـلُ الـصَّـلَاةِ وَ الـزَّكَـاةِ وَ تَـفْـسِـيـرُ الـتَّـوْحِـيـدِ قَـوْلُـهُ تَـعَـالَـى : ﴿ وَمَآ أُمِرُوٓاْ إِلَّا لِيَعْبُدُواْ ٱللَّهَ مُخْلِصِينَ لَهُ ٱلدِّينَ حُنَفَآءَ وَيُقِيمُواْ ٱلصَّلَوٰةَ وَيُؤْتُواْ ٱلزَّكَوٰةَۚ وَذَٰلِكَ دِينُ ٱلْقَيِّمَةِ ٥ ﴾ وَ دَلِـيـلُ الـصِّـيَـامِ قَـوْلُـهُ تَـعَـالَـى : ﴿ يَـٰٓأَيُّهَا ٱلَّذِينَ ءَامَنُواْ كُتِبَ عَلَيْكُمُ ٱلصِّيَامُ كَمَا كُتِبَ عَلَى ٱلَّذِينَ مِن قَبْلِكُمْ لَعَلَّكُمْ تَتَّقُونَ ١٨٣ ﴾ وَ دَلِـيـلُ الْـحَـجِّ قَـوْلُـهُ تَـعَـالَـى : ﴿ وَلِلَّهِ عَلَى ٱلنَّاسِ حِجُّ ٱلْبَيْتِ مَنِ ٱسْتَطَاعَ إِلَيْهِ سَبِيلًاۚ وَمَن كَفَرَ فَإِنَّ ٱللَّهَ غَنِيٌّ عَنِ ٱلْعَـٰلَمِينَ ٩٧ ﴾

"The second principle is knowing the religion of Islām with proofs. Islām is to submit to Allāh with Tawhīd, yield to Him with obedience, and the disavowing Shirk.

It (the religion of Islām) has three levels: Islām, ʾĪmān (faith), and Ihsān. Each level has its own pillars.

The first level (Islām)

has five pillars:

1-Testifying that there is no deity worthy of worship in truth but Allāh, and that Muḥammad is His Messenger.

2-Performing Ṣalāh

3-Paying the Zakat

4-Fasting the month of Ramaḍān.

5-Pilgrimage to the Sacred House (Mecca).

The evidence for testimony of faith is His (سُبْحَانَهُ وَتَعَالَى) saying, "There is no god but He: That is the witness of Allāh, His angels, and those endued with knowledge. Standing firm on justice. There is no god but He, the Exalted in Power, the Wise." [Sūrah ʾĀli ʿImrān 3:18]

This means that it is only Allāh that is worthy of being worshipped, and the negation, "... no deity ", implies the denial of any other deities worshipped besides Allāh who has no partners in the worship of

Him just as He has no partners in His Domain. The following verses illustrate this point,

"Behold! Abraham said to his father and his people: 'I do indeed clear myself of what you worship: (I worship) only Him Who originated me, and He will certainly guide me.' And he left it as a Word to endure among those who came after him, that they may turn back (to Allāh)." [Sūrah az-Zukhruf 43:26-28]

His saying, "Say: 'O People of the Book! come to common terms as between us and you: That we worship none but Allāh; that we associate no partners with him; that we erect not, from among ourselves, Rabb (Cherisher and Sustainer) and patrons other than Allāh.' If then they turn back, say ye: "Bear witness that we (at least) are Muslims (bowing to Allāh's Will)." [Sūrah ʾĀli ʿImrān 3:64]

The evidence for testifying that Muḥammad (صَلَّى ٱللَّهُ عَلَيْهِ وَسَلَّمَ) is the Messenger of Allāh is in His (سُبْحَانَهُ وَتَعَالَىٰ) saying, "Now has come unto you a Messenger from amongst yourselves: it grieves him that you should suffer, ardently anxious is he over you: to the Believers is he most kind and merciful. But if they turn away, say: '(Allāh) suffices me: there

is no god but He: On Him is my trust, - He the Rabb (Cherisher and Sustainer) of the Throne Supreme!'" [Sūrah at-Tawbah 9:128-129]

The meaning of testifying that Muḥammad (صَلَّىٰٱللَّهُعَلَيْهِوَسَلَّمَ) is the Messenger of Allāh signifies that one should obey his ordinances, believe him in what he tells, avoid what he prohibits, and to only worship Allāh according to what has been legislated. The evidence for Ṣalāh, Zakat, and an explanation of Tawhīd is in His (سُبْحَانَهُۥوَتَعَالَىٰ) saying, "And they have been commanded no more than this: to worship Allāh, offering Him sincere devotion, being true (in faith); to establish regular prayer; and to give Zakat; and that is the Religion Right and Straight." [Sūrah al-Bayyinah 98:5]

The evidence for fasting is His (سُبْحَانَهُۥوَتَعَالَىٰ) saying, "O you who believe! Fasting is prescribed to you as it was prescribed to those before you, that you may (learn) self-restraint." [al-Baqarah 2:183]

The evidence for Ḥajj (Pilgrimage) is His (سُبْحَانَهُۥوَتَعَالَىٰ) saying, "Pilgrimage thereto is a duty man owe to Allāh, - those who can afford the journey; but if any deny faith, Allāh stands not in need of any of His creatures." [Sūrah ʾĀli ʿImrān 3:97]

Explanation

This is the second fundamental principle which knowing the religion of Islām which has three levels. The Messenger of Allāh (صَلَّى ٱللَّهُ عَلَيْهِ وَسَلَّمَ) has explained them. The first is Islām in which is having sincere devotion to Allāh alone. Meaning submit to Allāh through worship, making that worship exclusively for Him and no other, and disavowing yourself from Shirk and its people.

So, when the servant does that he has submitted. Meaning, he has yielded and humbled himself to none besides Allāh through worship. He has also disavowed himself from Shirk and its people. Allāh (سُبْحَانَهُ وَتَعَالَىٰ) says,

﴿ فَمَن يَكْفُرْ بِٱلطَّٰغُوتِ وَيُؤْمِنۢ بِٱللَّهِ فَقَدِ ٱسْتَمْسَكَ بِٱلْعُرْوَةِ ٱلْوُثْقَىٰ ﴾

> **"Whoever disbelieves in Tāghūt and believes in Allāh, then he has grasped the most trustworthy handhold that will never break. And Allāh is All-Hearer, All-Knower."** [*Sūrah al-Baqarah* 2:256]

Disbelieving in the Tāghūt (false deities) is to disavowal oneself from Shirk and its people, reject of Shirk, and belief that it is false. There is the level of ʾĪmān, and Ihsān. All of which under Islām. The religion which Allāh has legislated for His servants and has sent the messengers conveying it (Islām).. The level of Islām includes actions performed with the body.

Islām has 5 pillars which are the following:

- testifying that there is no deity worthy of worship in truth except Allāh and that Muḥammad is the messenger of Allāh,
- Ṣalāh,
- performing zakat,
- fasting the month of Ramaḍān,
- pilgrimage to the house of Allāh {Kʿabah} to whoever is capable of it.

All of this just as the Prophet (صَلَّى ٱللَّهُ عَلَيْهِ وَسَلَّمَ) said,

بُنِيَ الْإِسْلَامُ عَلَى خَمْسٍ : شَهَادَةِ أَنْ لَا إِلَهَ إِلَّا اللهُ ، وَ أَنَّ مُـحَمَّدًا رَسُولُ اللهِ ، وَ إِقَامِ الصَّلَاةِ ، وَ إِيتَاءِ الزَّكَاةِ ، وَ صَوْمِ رَمَضَانَ ، وَ حَجِّ الْبَيْتِ

"al-Islām is raised on five (pillars), testifying that there is no deity worthy of worship in truth except Allāh, that Muḥammad is His slave and messenger, and the establishment of Ṣalāh, payment of Zakat, Pilgrimage to the House (Ka'ba) and the fast of Ramaḍān."[8]

So, the first pillar of Islām is the testimony that none has the right to be worshiped in truth except Allāh. One enters the religion of Islām upon saying it. When he testifies that there is no deity deserves to be worshiped but Allāh, it means that nothing is worthy to be worshipped but Allāh. This statement contains a negation as well as an affirmation. The statement, **"there is no deity"** is the negation and the statement, **"but Allāh"** is the affirmation. Allāh (سُبْحَانَهُ وَتَعَالَىٰ) says,

[8] Ḥadīth of Ibn ʿUmar (رَضِيَ ٱللَّهُ عَنْهُمَا) collected by al-Bukhārī No. (8) and by Muslim No. (16).

﴿ إِيَّاكَ نَعۡبُدُ وَإِيَّاكَ نَسۡتَعِينُ ۝٥ ﴾

"You (Alone) we worship, and You (Alone) we ask for help (for each and everything)." [*Sūrah al-Fatihah* 1:5]

He (سُبۡحَانَهُۥ وَتَعَالَىٰ) also says,

﴿ وَمَآ أُمِرُوٓاْ إِلَّا لِيَعۡبُدُواْ ٱللَّهَ مُخۡلِصِينَ لَهُ ٱلدِّينَ حُنَفَآءَ ﴾

"And they were commanded not, but that they should worship Allāh, and worship none but Him Alone." [*Sūrah Bayyinah* 98:5]

He (سُبۡحَانَهُۥ وَتَعَالَىٰ) also said,

﴿ ذَٰلِكَ بِأَنَّ ٱللَّهَ هُوَ ٱلۡحَقُّ وَأَنَّ مَا يَدۡعُونَ مِن دُونِهِۦ هُوَ ٱلۡبَٰطِلُ ﴾

"That is because Allāh He is the Truth (the only True Deity of all that exists, Who has no partners or rivals with Him), and what they (the polytheists) invoke besides Him, it is Bātil (falsehood)." [Sūrah al-Ḥajj 22:62]

As for one saying the testimony of faith without implementing it will not benefit., For instance, it is like one saying, "there is no deity worthy of worship except Allāh", but he does not exclusively worship Allāh alone. His testimony of faith carries no benefit just like the hypocrites. they say the testimony of faith yet they don't believe in it. that's the reason why they are in the lowest level of hell. So, the person that says, "there is no deity worthy of worship except Allāh" then worships graves and idols, will not benefit him and his testimony of faith is futile.

As for the second testimony of faith which is saying. "I bear witness that Muḥammad is the Messenger of Allāh". the proof of that is Allāh's (سُبْحَانَهُ وَتَعَالَىٰ) statement,

﴿ لَقَدْ جَآءَكُمْ رَسُولٌ مِّنْ أَنفُسِكُمْ ﴾

"Verily, there has come unto you a Messenger (Muḥammad صَلَّى ٱللَّٰهُ عَلَيْهِ وَسَلَّمَ) from amongst yourselves." [*Sūrah at-Tawbah* 9:128]

Muḥammad (صَلَّى ٱللَّٰهُ عَلَيْهِ وَسَلَّمَ) is known to you because he is from amongst you. He comes from the most honorable of tribes amongst Bani Hāshim,

﴿ عَزِيزٌ عَلَيۡهِ مَا عَنِتُّمۡ ﴾

"It grieves him that you should receive any injury or difficulty." [*Sūrah at-Tawbah* 9:128]

Meaning, it is hard on him what is hard on you.

﴿ حَرِيصٌ عَلَيۡكُم ﴾

"is anxious over you" being guided and being saved from hell.

Allāh (سُبۡحَانَهُۥ وَتَعَالَىٰ) says,

﴿ مُّحَمَّدٌ رَّسُولُ ٱللَّهِۚ ﴾

"Muḥammad (صَلَّى ٱللَّهُ عَلَيۡهِ وَسَلَّمَ) is the Messenger of Allāh)." [*Sūrah Fath* 48:29]

After making this testimony one must obey him (the Prophet) in what he ordered, believe in what he said, stay away from what he forbidden, and only worship Allāh with what he has legislated.

So, these four matters are mandatory:

First: obeying him in what he ordered from the Ṣalāh, Zakat, and so forth.

Second: believing what he said about the hereafter, paradise, hell, and so forth.

Third: avoiding what he forbidden us from like fornicating, Ribā, and so forth from what Allāh and His Messenger prohibited.

Forth: only worship Allāh with what he legislated. So, one mustn't introduce in the religion what Allāh has not legislated. This is based upon the statement of Prophet (صَلَّى ٱللَّهُ عَلَيْهِ وَسَلَّمَ),

مَنْ عَمِلَ عَمَلاً لَيْسَ عَلَيْهِ أَمْرُنَا فَهُوَ رَدٌّ

"He who did any act for which there is no sanction from our behalf, it will be rejected."[9]

And in another version,

مَنْ أَحْدَثَ فِي أَمْرِنَا هَذَا مَا لَيْسَ مِنْهُ فَهُوَ رَدٌّ

[9] Collected by Muslim No. (1718) and al-Bukhārī No. (7349 & 7350).

"He who innovates things in our affairs for which there is no valid (reason) (commits sin) is to be rejected."[10]

Meaning, it will be denied.

The proof of the Ṣalāh, Zakat, and Tafsīr of Tawhīd is what Allāh (سُبْحَانَهُ وَتَعَالَىٰ) says,

﴿ وَمَآ أُمِرُوٓاْ إِلَّا لِيَعۡبُدُواْ ٱللَّهَ مُخۡلِصِينَ لَهُ ٱلدِّينَ حُنَفَآءَ ﴾

"And they were commanded not, but that they should worship Allāh and none but Him Alone)."

This is the Tafsīr of Tawhīd.

﴿ وَيُقِيمُواْ ٱلصَّلَوٰةَ وَيُؤۡتُواْ ٱلزَّكَوٰةَۚ وَذَٰلِكَ دِينُ ٱلۡقَيِّمَةِ ۝٥ ﴾

"and perform As-Ṣalāh (Iqamat-as-Ṣalāh) and give Zakat: and that is the right religion." [*Sūrah al-Bayyinah* 98:5]

He (سُبْحَانَهُ وَتَعَالَىٰ) says,

---

[10] Collected by al-Bukhārī No. (2697) and Muslim No. (1718) from the Ḥadīth of ʿĀʾishah (رَضِيَ ٱللَّهُ عَنْهَا).

﴿ فَإِن تَابُوا۟ وَأَقَامُوا۟ ٱلصَّلَوٰةَ وَءَاتَوُا۟ ٱلزَّكَوٰةَ فَإِخْوَٰنُكُمْ فِى ٱلدِّينِ ۗ ﴾

"But if they repent, perform As-Salat (Iqamat-as-Salat) and give Zakat, then they are your brethren in religion." [*Sūrah at-Tawbah* 9:11]

He (سُبْحَانَهُ وَتَعَالَى) also says,

﴿ فَإِن تَابُوا۟ وَأَقَامُوا۟ ٱلصَّلَوٰةَ وَءَاتَوُا۟ ٱلزَّكَوٰةَ فَخَلُّوا۟ سَبِيلَهُمْ ۚ ﴾

"But if they repent and perform As-Salat (Iqamat-as-Salat), and give Zakat, then leave their way free." [*Sūrah at-Tawbah* 9:5]

The proof of fasting, Allāh (سُبْحَانَهُ وَتَعَالَى) says,

﴿ يَٰٓأَيُّهَا ٱلَّذِينَ ءَامَنُوا۟ كُتِبَ عَلَيْكُمُ ٱلصِّيَامُ كَمَا كُتِبَ عَلَى ٱلَّذِينَ مِن قَبْلِكُمْ ﴾

"O you who believe! Observing As-Saum (the fasting) is prescribed for you as it was prescribed for those before you." [*Sūrah al-Baqarah* 2:183]

Until His statement (سُبْحَانَهُوَتَعَالَى),

﴿ شَهْرُ رَمَضَانَ ﴾

"The month of Ramaḍān" [*Sūrah al-Baqarah* 2:185]

Meaning fasting is obligatory on you every year in the month of Ramaḍān.

the proof of Hajj is the statement of Allāh (سُبْحَانَهُوَتَعَالَى),

﴿ وَلِلَّهِ عَلَى ٱلنَّاسِ حِجُّ ٱلْبَيْتِ مَنِ ٱسْتَطَاعَ إِلَيْهِ سَبِيلًا ﴾

"And Hajj (pilgrimage to Makkah) to the House (Ka'bah) is a duty that mankind owes to Allāh, those who can afford the expenses." [*Sūrah ʾĀli ʿImrān* 3:97]

It must be performed once in a lifetime, the Prophet (صَلَّىٱللَّهُعَلَيْهِوَسَلَّمَ) said,

الْـحَجُّ مَرَّةٌ ، فَمَنْ زَادَ فَهُوَ تَطَوُّعٌ

"Only once, and if anyone performs it more often, he performs a supererogatory act."[11]

These are the five pillars of Islām.

[11] Collected by Imām ʾAḥmad No. (1/255, 290, 352, 370, & 371); and Collected by Abū Dāwud in his Sunan No. (1721); and an-Nisāʾi No. (2619); and Ibn Maajah No. (2886); and collected by al-Haakim No. (1728).

The author (رَحِمَهُ ٱللَّهُ) said,

الْـمَـرْتَـبَـةُ الـثَّـانِـيَـةُ : الْإِيـمَـانُ . وَ هُـوَ بِـضْـعٌ وَ سَـبْـعُـونَ شُـعْـبَـةً , فَـأَعْـلَاهَـا قَـوْلُ (لَا إِلَـهَ إِلَّا اللهُ) , وَ أَدْنَـاهَـا إِمَـاطَـةُ الْأَذَى عَـنِ الـطَّـرِيـقِ , وَ الْـحَـيَـاءُ شُـبْـعَـةٌ مِـنَ الْإِيـمَـانِ . وَ أَرْكَـانُـهُ سِـتَّـةٌ : أَنْ تُـؤْمِـنَ بِـاللهِ , وَ مَـلَائِـكَـتِـهِ , وَ كُـتُـبِـهِ , وَ رَسُـلِـهِ , وَ الْـيَـوْمِ الْآخِـرِ , وَ تُـؤْمِـنَ بِـالْـقَـدَرِ خَـيْـرِهِ وَ شَـرِّهِ . وَ الـدَّلِـيـلُ عَـلَـى هَـذِهِ الْأَرْكَـانِ الـسِّـتَـةِ قَـوْلُـهُ تَـعَـالَـى : ﴿ ۞ لَّيْسَ ٱلْبِرَّ أَن تُوَلُّوا۟ وُجُوهَكُمْ قِبَلَ ٱلْمَشْرِقِ وَٱلْمَغْرِبِ وَلَٰكِنَّ ٱلْبِرَّ مَنْ ءَامَنَ بِٱللَّهِ وَٱلْيَوْمِ ٱلْـَٔاخِرِ وَٱلْمَلَٰٓئِكَةِ وَٱلْكِتَٰبِ وَٱلنَّبِيِّـۧنَ ﴾ وَ دَلِـيـلُ الْـقَـدَرِ قَـوْلُـهُ تَـعَـالَـى : ﴿ إِنَّا كُلَّ شَىْءٍ خَلَقْنَٰهُ بِقَدَرٍ ﴿٤٩﴾ ﴾ الْـمَـرْتَـبَـةُ الـثَّـالِـثَـةُ : (الْإِحْـسَـانُ) : رُكْـنٌ وَاحِـدٌ , وَ هُـوَ أَنْ تَـعْـبُـدَ اللهَ كَـأَنَّـكَ تَـرَاهُ , فَـإِنْ لَـمْ تَـكُـنْ تَـرَاهُ فَـإِنَّـهُ يَـرَاكَ . وَ الـدَّلِـيـلُ قَـوْلُـهُ تَـعَـالَـى : ﴿ إِنَّ ٱللَّهَ مَعَ ٱلَّذِينَ ٱتَّقَوا۟ وَّٱلَّذِينَ هُم مُّحْسِنُونَ ﴿١٢٨﴾ ﴾ وَ قَوْلُهُ ﴿ وَتَوَكَّلْ عَلَى ٱلْعَزِيزِ ٱلرَّحِيمِ ﴿٢١٧﴾ ٱلَّذِى يَرَىٰكَ حِينَ تَقُومُ ﴿٢١٨﴾ وَتَقَلُّبَكَ فِى ٱلسَّٰجِدِينَ ﴿٢١٩﴾ إِنَّهُۥ هُوَ

ٱلسَّمِيعُ ٱلْعَلِيمُ ﴿٢٢٠﴾ ﴾ وَقَوْلُهُ تَعَالَى : ﴿ وَمَا تَكُونُ فِي شَأْنٍ وَمَا تَتْلُواْ مِنْهُ مِن قُرْءَانٍ وَلَا تَعْمَلُونَ مِنْ عَمَلٍ إِلَّا كُنَّا عَلَيْكُمْ شُهُودًا إِذْ تُفِيضُونَ فِيهِ ﴾

"The second level is ʾĪmān (Faith)

ʾĪmān comprises of seventy and some odd branches, that highest is to say "lā ilaha illa Allāh" which is to testify that "there is no deity worthy of worshiped except Allāh", and the lowest branch is to remove obstacles from the path of the people. Modesty is one of the branches of ʾĪmān. The pillars of ʾĪmān are six:

Belief in Allāh, His Angles, His Books, His Messengers, The Last Day, and Divine Decree, whether good or bad. Evidence for the six pillars of ʾĪmān is,

"It is not righteousness that you turn your faces towards East or West; but it is righteousness to believe in Allāh and the Last Day, and the Angels, and the Book, and the Messengers; to spend of your substance, out of love for Him, for your kin, for orphans, for the needy, for the wayfarer, for those

who ask, and for the ransom of slaves; to be steadfast in prayer, and give Zakat; to fulfill the contracts which you have made; and to be firm and patient, in pain (or suffering) and adversity, and throughout all periods of panic. Such are the people of truth, the God fearing." [Sūrah al-Baqarah 2:177]

Evidence for Divine Decree is Allāh's (سُبْحَانَهُ وَتَعَالَى) statement,

"Verily, all things have We created in proportion and measure." [Sūrah al-Qamar 54:49]

The third level is Ihsān

Ihsān has only one pillar which is to worship Allāh as though you see Him; for if you do not see Him, indeed He sees you.

Evidence for Ihsān is Allah's statement, "For Allāh is with those who restrain themselves, and those who do good." [Sūrah an-Nahl 16:128]

Also His saying, "In whatever business you may be, and whatever portion you may be reciting from the Qur'ān, - and whatever deed you (mankind) may be doing, - We are Witnesses thereof when you are deeply engrossed therein." [Sūrah Yūnus 10:61]

Explanation

ʾĪmān is associated with the heart as it relates to believing in Allāh, He is the Lord of all creation, He is worthy of worship, believe in the angels, His books, His messengers, resurrection after death, belief in hell and paradise, and belief in Divine Decree, the good and bad of it.

All of these beliefs are associate with the heart. This is one of the foundations which is imperative. So, there is no Islām without ʾĪmān and vice versa. So, both are important. Submission of physical actions and the heart as well belief in the heart is obligatory. Based upon this Allāh combined both, Islām & ʾĪmān, in His Great book, and the Messenger (صَلَّى ٱللَّهُ عَلَيْهِ وَسَلَّمَ) mentioned them both as well.

So, Islām is physical submission through obedience to Allāh and abandoning acts of disobedience. ʾĪmān includes actions in the heart and believe in the heart. The word 'Islām' can be applied to the word 'ʾĪmān' and vice versa.

So, if ʾĪmān is mentioned it includes everything (Islām & ʾĪmān) and if Islām is mentioned it includes both. Allāh (سُبْحَانَهُ وَتَعَالَىٰ) says,

﴿ إِنَّ ٱلدِّينَ عِندَ ٱللَّهِ ٱلْإِسْلَٰمُ ﴾

"Truly, the religion with Allāh is Islām." [*Sūrah ʾĀli ʿImrān* 3:19]

So, it includes everything, the inward as well as outward actions.

The same can be said for ʾĪmān which when mentioned it is applied to both. Based upon this the Prophet (صَلَّى ٱللَّهُ عَلَيْهِ وَسَلَّمَ) said,

الإِيمَانُ بِضْعٌ وَسَبْعُونَ أَوْ بِضْعٌ وَسِتُّونَ شُعْبَةً فَأَفْضَلُهَا قَوْلُ لاَ إِلَهَ إِلاَّ اللَّهُ وَأَدْنَاهَا إِمَاطَةُ الأَذَى عَنِ الطَّرِيقِ

"Faith has over seventy branches or over sixty branches. The loftiest branch is the declaration that there is no deity worthy of worship except Allāh, and the lowest is the removal of harm from the path."

So, ʾĪmān here includes everything. It includes the pillars of Islām, the physical actions, just as it also includes inward actions and Ihsān.

As for ʾIḥsān, it is a perfection of physical and spiritual worship which one worships Allāh as if you see him, and if you don't see Him He sees you. So, whoever worships Allāh with this level of awareness has reached the level of ʾIḥsān and has attain all levels of good just as Allāh (سُبْحَانَهُۥ وَتَعَالَىٰ) says,

﴿ إِنَّ ٱللَّهَ مَعَ ٱلَّذِينَ ٱتَّقَوا۟ وَّٱلَّذِينَ هُم مُّحْسِنُونَ ١٢٨ ﴾

"Truly, Allāh is with those who fear Him (keep their duty unto Him), and those who are Muhsinūn (good-doers, - see the footnote of V.9:120)." [*Sūrah An-Nahl* 16:128]

He (عَزَّوَجَلَّ) also says,

﴿ إِنَّ رَحْمَتَ ٱللَّهِ قَرِيبٌ مِّنَ ٱلْمُحْسِنِينَ ٥٦ ﴾

"Surely, Allāh's Mercy is (ever) near unto the good doers." [*Sūrah al-ʿArāf* 7:56]

These verses with this connotation are numerous.

The author (رَحِمَهُ ٱللَّهُ) said,

وَالدَّلِيلُ مِنَ السَّنَّةِ: حَدِيثُ جِبْرَائِيلَ الْمَشْهُورِ، عَنْ عُمَرَ (رَضِيَ اللهُ عَنْهُ) قَالَ: ((بَيْنَمَا نَحْنُ جُلُوسٌ عِنْدَ رَسُولِ اللهِ (صَلَّى اللهُ عَلَيْهِ وَ سَلَّمَ) ذَاتَ يَوْمٍ إِذْ طَلَعَ عَلَيْنَا رَجُلٌ: شَدِيدُ بَيَاضِ الثِّيَابِ، شَدِيدُ سَوَادِ الشَّعْرِ، لَا يُرَى عَلَيْهِ أَثَرُ السَّفَرِ، وَ لَا يَعْرِفُهُ مِنَّا أَحَدٌ، حَتَّى جَلَسَ إِلَى النَّبِيِّ (صَلَّى اللهُ عَلَيْهِ وَ سَلَّمَ)، فَأَسْنَدَ رُكْبَتَيْهِ إِلَى رُكْبَتَيْهِ، وَ وَضَعَ كَفَّيْهِ عَلَى فَخِذَيْهِ. وَ قَالَ: يَا مُحَمَّدُ، أَخْبِرْنِي عَنِ الْإِسْلَامِ؟ فَقَالَ رَسُولُ اللهِ (صَلَّى اللهُ عَلَيْهِ وَ سَلَّمَ): الْإِسْلَامُ أَنْ تَشْهَدَ أَنْ لَا إِلَهَ إِلَّا اللهُ، وَ أَنَّ مُحَمَّداً رَسُولُ اللهِ، وَ تُقِيمَ الصَّلَاةَ، وَ تُؤْتِيَ الزَّكَاةَ، وَ تَصُومَ رَمَضَانَ، وَ تَحُجَّ الْبَيْتَ إِنِ اسْتَطَعْتَ إِلَيْهِ سَبِيلاً. قَالَ: صَدَقْتَ. فَعَجِبْنَا لَهُ يَسْأَلُهُ وَ يُصَدِّقُهُ. قَالَ: فَأَخْبِرْنِي عَنِ الْإِيمَانِ

؟ قَـالَ : أَنْ تُـؤْمِـنَ بِـاللهِ , وَ مَـلَائِـكَـتِـهِ , وَ كُـتُـبِـهِ , وَ رُسُـلِـهِ , وَالْـيَـوْمِ الْآخِـرِ , وَ بِـالْـقَـدَرِ خَـيْـرِهِ وَ شَـرِّهِ. قَـالَ : صَـدَقْـتَ , قَـالَ : فَـأَخْـبِـرْنِـي عَـنِ الْإِحْـسَـانِ ؟ قَـالَ : أَنْ تَـعْـبُـدَ اللهَ كَـأَنَّـكَ تَـرَاهُ , فَـإِنْ لَـمْ تَـكُـنْ تَـرَاهُ فَـإِنَّـهُ يَـرَاكَ . قَـالَ : فَـأَخْـبِـرْنِـي عَـنِ الـسَّـاعَـةِ ؟ قَـالَ : مَـا الْـمَـسْـئُـولُ عَـنْـهَـا بِـأَعْـلَـمَ مِـنَ الـسَّـائِـلِ !! قَـالَ : أَخْـبِـرْنِـي عَـنْ أَمَـارَاتِـهَـا ؟ قَـالَ : أَنْ تَـلِـدَ الْأَمَـةُ رَبَّـتَـهَـا , وَأَنْ تَـرَى الْـحُـفَـاةَ الْـعُـرَاةَ الْـعَـالَـةَ رِعَـاءَ الـشَّـاةِ يَـتَـطَـاوَلُـونَ فِـي الْـبُـنْـيَـانِ. قَـالَ : فَـمَـضَـى , فَـلَـبِـثْـنَـا مَـلِـيًّـا , فَـقَـالَ : يَـا عُـمَـرُ , أَتَـدْرِي مَـنِ الـسَّـائِـلُ ؟ قُـلْـتُ : اللهُ وَ رَسُـولُـهُ أَعْـلَـمُ . قَـالَ : هَـذَا جِـبْـرِيـلُ أَتَـاكُـمْ يُـعَـلِّـمُـكُـمْ أَمْـرَ دِيـنِـكُـمْ .))

Evidence from the Sunanh is the well-known Hadith of Jibrīl (Gabriel).

"According to Umar bin Al-Khattab, may Allāh be pleased with him, who said:

"One day while we were sitting with the Prophet, (صَلَّى ٱللَّهُ عَلَيْهِ وَسَلَّمَ) there came upon us a man with very white clothes and very dark hair; no traces of any traveling on him, and none of us knew him. He sat before the Prophet (صَلَّى ٱللَّهُ عَلَيْهِ وَسَلَّمَ) with his knees touching the Prophet's knees, and his hands over the Prophet's thighs. The stranger said:

"O Muḥammad, tell me about Islām." He (صَلَّى ٱللَّهُ عَلَيْهِ وَسَلَّمَ) said: "It is to testify that there is no deity worthy of worship except Allāh and that Muḥammad is the Messenger of Allāh, to perform prayer, to give Zakat, to fast the month of Ramaḍān, and to perform the Pilgrimage to the House, if you can afford it.". He (the stranger) said: "You have spoken the truth." We wondered why he asked him and then told him that what he had said was true.

The stranger then said: "Tell me about ʾĪmān." He said: "It is to believe in Allāh, His Angles, His Books, His Messengers, The Last Day, and in Destiny, whether good or bad."

He said: "Tell me about Ihsan." He said: "To worship Allāh as if you are seeing Him, for though you do not see Him, He sees you."

He said: "Tell me about the Final Day." He said: "The answerer has no better knowledge than the questioner."

He said: "Tell me about its signs." He said: "When a slave girl gives birth to her own mistress, and when you see the bare-footed and tattered needy shepherds vying with each other in erecting high buildings."

Then that stranger left, and the Prophet was silent for a while then said: "O Omar, do you know who was the questioner?" I said:" Allāh and His Messenger know better." He said: "That was Gabriel. He came to teach you your religion."

THE THIRD PRINCIPLE: KNOWING THE PROPHET

The author (رَحِمَهُ ٱللَّهُ) said,

الْأَصْلُ الثَّالِثُ: مَعْرِفَةُ نَبِيِّكُمْ (صَلَّى اللهُ عَلَيْهِ وَ سَلَّمَ), وَ هُوَ مُحَمَّدٌ بْنُ عَبْدِ اللهِ بْنِ عَبْدِ الْمُطَّلِّبِ بْنِ هَاشِمٍ, وَ هَاشِمٌ مِنْ قُرَيْشٍ, وَ قُرَيْشٌ مِنَ الْعَرَبِ , وَالْعَرَبُ مِنْ ذُرِيَّةِ إِسْمَاعِيلَ بْنِ إِبْرَاهِيمَ الْخَلِيلِ, عَلَيْهِ وَ عَلَى نَبِيِّنَا أَفْضَلُ الصَّلَاةِ وَ السَّلَامِ. وَ لَهُ مِنَ الْعُمْرِ ثَلَاثٌ وَ سِتُّونَ سَنَةً, مِنْهَا أَرْبَعُونَ قَبْلَ النُّبُوَّةِ وَ ثَلَاثٌ وَ عِشْرُونَ نَبِيّاً وَ رَسُولاً. نُبِّيءَ بـ﴿ٱقْرَأْ﴾ وَ أُرْسِلَ بـ﴿ٱلْمُدَّثِّرُ﴾.

وَ بَلَدُهُ مَكَّةُ , وَهَاجَرَ إِلَى الْمَدِينَةِ بَعَثَهُ اللهُ بِالنَّذَارَةِ عَنِ الشِّرْكِ , وَ يَدْعُو إِلَى التَّوْحِيدِ . وَ الدَّلِيلُ قَوْلُهُ تَعَالَى : ﴿ يَٰٓأَيُّهَا ٱلْمُدَّثِّرُ ﴿١﴾ قُمْ فَأَنذِرْ ﴿٢﴾ وَرَبَّكَ فَكَبِّرْ ﴿٣﴾ وَثِيَابَكَ فَطَهِّرْ ﴿٤﴾ وَٱلرُّجْزَ فَٱهْجُرْ ﴿٥﴾ وَلَا تَمْنُن تَسْتَكْثِرُ ﴿٦﴾ وَلِرَبِّكَ فَٱصْبِرْ ﴿٧﴾ ﴾ وَ مَعْنَى : ﴿ قُمْ فَأَنذِرْ ﴾ : يَنْذُرُ عَنِ الشِّرْكِ وَ يَدْعُو إِلَى التَّوْحِيدِ . ﴿ وَرَبَّكَ فَكَبِّرْ ﴿٣﴾ ﴾ : أَيْ : عَظِّمْكَ بِالتَّوْحِيدِ . ﴿ وَثِيَابَكَ فَطَهِّرْ ﴿٤﴾ ﴾ : أَيْ : طَهِّرْ أَعْمَالَكَ عَنِ الشِّرْكِ . ﴿ وَٱلرُّجْزَ فَٱهْجُرْ ﴿٥﴾ ﴾ : الرُّجْزُ : الْأَصْنَامُ , وَ هَجْرُهَا تَرْكُهَا وَ الْبَرَاءَةُ مِنْهَا وَ مِنْ أَهْلِهَا . أَخَذَ عَلَى هَذَا عَشْرَ سِنِينَ يَدْعُو إِلَى التَّوْحِيدِ . وَ بَعْدَ الْعَشْرِ عُرِجَ بِهِ إِلَى السَّمَاءِ , وَ فُرِضَتْ عَلَيْهِ الصَّلَوَاتُ الْخَمْسُ , وَ صَلَّى فِي مَكَّةَ ثَلَاثَ سِنِينَ . وَ بَعْدَهَا أُمِرَ بِالْهِجْرَةِ إِلَى الْمَدِينَةِ .

"The Third Fundamental is knowing your Prophet Muḥammad (ﷺ).

He is Muḥammad, the son of ʿAbdullāh, the son of ʿAbdul Muttalib, the son of Hāshim, and Hāshim is from Quraysh; and Quraysh from the Arabs. The Arabs are the descendants of Ismaeel, the son Ibrāhīm Al-Khalīl. He was born in Mecca and lived for sixty-three years. Forty years before becoming a Prophet and he was a prophet and messenger for twenty-three years.

He was initiated into prophethood with the revelation of,

"Read!" [Sūrah al-Alaq 96:1]

He was made a Messenger with revelation of, "al-Mudathir. "

Mecca was his country. Allāh sent him as a messenger to warn against associating partners with Allāh and call (people) to the Tawhīd of Allāh. The evidence is in His (سُبۡحَانَهُۥوَتَعَالَىٰ) statement,

"O you (Muḥammad ﷺ) enveloped (in garments)! Arise and warn! And your Lord (Allāh) magnify! And your garments purify! And keep away from *Ar-Rujz* (the idols)! And give not a thing in order to have more (or consider not your deeds of

Allah's obedience as a favor to Allah). And be patient for the sake of your Lord (i.e. perform your duty to Allāh)." [Sūrah al-Mudathir 74:1-7]

The statement, "Arise and warn!" means warn against Shirk and call the people to Tawhīd. The statement, "And your Lord (Allāh) magnify!" refers to venerating Him (Allāh) through Tawhīd. The statement, "And your garments purify!" refers to keeping your deeds clean from Shirk. The statement, "And keep away from *Ar-Rujz* (the idols)!" refers to staying away from idols, idolaters, and disavowal oneself from them.

He continued calling to Tawhīd for ten years. Afterward, he was ascended to Heaven where the five prayers (Ṣalāh) and their times were made a religious obligation. Thus, he performed the Ṣalāh in Mecca for three years. Then he was ordered to migrate to Madīnah.

Explanation

This is the third fundamental principle which is knowing our Prophet (صَلَّى ٱللَّٰهُ عَلَيْهِ وَسَلَّمَ). So, knowing about one's Prophet whom Allāh sent, conveyed Islām, clarified the legislation which Allāh has ordered, and explained the worship we were created for is a religious duty upon all mankind.".

This Prophet is Muḥammad (صَلَّى ٱللَّٰهُ عَلَيْهِ وَسَلَّمَ),the seal of the prophets, Allāh's messenger to this nation of Jinn and mankind whom Allāh sent him to all people. Allāh (سُبْحَانَهُ وَتَعَالَىٰ) says,

﴿ قُلْ يَٰٓأَيُّهَا ٱلنَّاسُ إِنِّى رَسُولُ ٱللَّهِ إِلَيْكُمْ جَمِيعًا ﴾

"Say (O Muḥammad صَلَّى ٱللَّٰهُ عَلَيْهِ وَسَلَّمَ): "O mankind! Verily, I am sent to you all as the Messenger of Allāh." [Sūrah al-ʿArāf 7:158]

He (سُبْحَانَهُ وَتَعَالَىٰ) also says,

﴿ وَمَآ أَرْسَلْنَٰكَ إِلَّا كَآفَّةً لِّلنَّاسِ بَشِيرًا وَنَذِيرًا ﴾

"And We have not sent you (O Muḥammad صَلَّى ٱللَّٰهُ عَلَيْهِ وَسَلَّمَ) except as a giver of glad tidings and a warner to all mankind." [Sūrah Saba 34:28]

He has several names among them are Muḥammad, ʾAḥmad, Al-Hāshir, and Al-Māḥī, and Al-Muqaffā. He was called these names because he is the seal of the prophets, the prophet of repentance, the prophet of mercy, and the prophet of fierce battle. All of these names belongs to him, however the most popular, superior, and greatest is Muḥammad. It is the same name that his family gave to him and is mentioned in the Qurʾān. Allāh (سُبْحَانَهُ وَتَعَالَىٰ) says,

﴿ مُّحَمَّدٌ رَّسُولُ ٱللَّهِ ﴾

> **"Muḥammad (صَلَّىٰ ٱللَّهُ عَلَيْهِ وَسَلَّمَ) is the Messenger of Allāh."** [Sūrah al-Fath 48:29]

The same is said for the name ʾAḥmad which ʿĪsā gave glad tidings to,

﴿ وَمُبَشِّرًا بِرَسُولٍ يَأْتِي مِنۢ بَعْدِي ٱسْمُهُۥٓ أَحْمَدُ ﴾

> **"and giving glad tidings of a Messenger to come after me, whose name shall be ʾAḥmad."** [*Sūrah as-Saff* 61:6]

He is Muḥammad, his father's name is ʿAbdullāh, his grandfather's name is ʿAbdul-Muttalib, and ʿAbdul-

Muttalib is a nickname for his real name which is Shaybah. His great grandfather's name is Hāshim and he was one of the chiefs of the Quraysh. ʿAbdul-Muttalib was also one of the leaders of Quraysh.

Hāshim was from Quraysh and Quraysh was a great Tribe. They were the best of the Arabs. The Prophet (صَلَّى ٱللَّهُ عَلَيْهِ وَسَلَّمَ) was among the elite of them, from Bani Hāshim. Bani Hāshim is from the best Quraysh. The founder's name was Fihr Ibn Mālik, yet some said that Quraysh is An-Nadr Ibn Kinānah, who is the grandfather of Fihr Ibn Mālik. The Quraysh are from the Arabs that originally weren't Arab. Their tongues were Arabize, so they spoke clear Arabic. They are actually more Arab than Qahtān (another tribe-originally Arabs). that's why it is said: there are two types of Arabs, those are the original Arabs and Arabized Arabs who are from the offspring of Ismaa'il Ibn Ibrāhīm (عَلَيْهِ ٱلصَّلَاةُ وَٱلسَّلَامُ).

This Great prophet, the prophet Muḥammad (صَلَّى ٱللَّهُ عَلَيْهِ وَسَلَّمَ) became a prophet with the revealing of, **"read"** which was among the first of what was revealed to him,

﴿ ٱقْرَأْ بِٱسْمِ رَبِّكَ ٱلَّذِى خَلَقَ ۝١ ﴾

"Read! In the Name of your Lord, Who has created (all that exists)." [*Sūrah al-ʿAlaq* 96:1]

With the revealing of this verse he became a prophet. Jibrīl came to him while he was in a cave, cave Hira, and made him read this Sūrah.

After a short period of time he arrived with Sūrah Al-Muddaththir, and he became a messenger with the verse,

﴿ يَٰٓأَيُّهَا ٱلْمُدَّثِّرُ ١ قُمْ فَأَنذِرْ ٢ ﴾

"O you (Muḥammad ﷺ) enveloped (in garments)! Arise and warn!" [*Sūrah Al-Muddaththir* 74:1-2]

The word **'Muddaththir'** refers to a person who is cover up in garments. After receiving the revelation it began weighty over him. So, he said to his family, "cover me up! cover me up! wrap me up! wrap me up!" due to the intense fear when Jibrīl (عَلَيْهِ ٱلصَّلَاةُ وَٱلسَّلَامُ) pressured him several times.

He, Jibrīl, said, **"read"** in preparation for the burden and weightiness of the message. then Allāh said,

﴿ يَٰٓأَيُّهَا ٱلْمُدَّثِّرُ ١ قُمْ فَأَنذِرْ ٢ ﴾

"O you (Muḥammad صَلَّىٱللَّهُعَلَيْهِوَسَلَّمَ) enveloped (in garments)! Arise and warn!" stand and warn the people. He became a messenger when he was ordered to warn (the people).

﴿ وَرَبَّكَ فَكَبِّرْ ۝٣ ﴾

"And your Lord (Allāh) magnify!" venerate Allāh through Tawhīd.

﴿ وَثِيَابَكَ فَطَهِّرْ ۝٤ ﴾

"And your garments purify!" Purify your deeds from Shirk. Purify your garments is not what is intended in this verse because the Ṣalāh was not made a religious duty at that time. Rather, what is intended here is one's deeds just as Allāh (سُبْحَانَهُوَتَعَالَىٰ) says,

﴿ وَلِبَاسُ ٱلتَّقْوَىٰ ذَٰلِكَ خَيْرٌ ﴾

> **"the raiment of righteousness, that is better."** [*Sūrah al-ʿArāf* 7:26]

So, deeds are also called raiment (i.e., clothes).

﴿ وَٱلرُّجۡزَ فَٱهۡجُرۡ ۝٥ ﴾

"And keep away from Ar-Rujz" the word "Rujz" refers to idols which are to be abandoned, left, and disavowal oneself from it and its people. He did this for ten years calling to Tawhīd, warning from Shirk, ordering to separate from worshiping anything besides Allāh, abandon the worship of idols. He also ordered them to single out Allāh alone in worship in their invocations , vows, sacrifices, and so forth.

After ten years he was ascended to the heavens with Jibrīl. The heavens were opened for him and reached a lofty place above the seventh heaven where he the creaking of the Pens. Allāh then announced to him speaking to the Prophet (صَلَّىٰ اللَّهُ عَلَيْهِ وَسَلَّمَ) directly where He made the five prayers a religious duty upon him. Originally it was fifty prayers afterward the he requested that it be lessened until Allāh made it five.

Then Allāh (سُبْحَانَهُ وَتَعَالَىٰ) said, they are five in number, yet they are fifty in the Preserved Tablet. Whoever maintains these five prayers and performs them (as legislated) will be written for him the reward of fifty. Because one good deed is multiplied tenfold.

Afterward, he came down with that(عَلَيْهِ ٱلصَّلَاةُ وَٱلسَّلَامُ) and it was the Ṣalāh was established five prayers throughout the day and night: Ẓuhr, ʿAsr, Maghrib, Ishaa, and Fajr. he performed them in Makkah for three years prior to migrating to al-Madīnah.

When the Quraysh increased in their harm and oppression to the Prophet (صَلَّى ٱللَّهُ عَلَيْهِ وَسَلَّمَ) and his Companions, Allāh allowed him to make Hijrah from Makkah to al-Madīnah. During the Ḥajj season the al-ʾAnsār pledged to the Prophet based upon him moving to them (in al-Madīnah) and them supporting and aiding him.

Upon the pledge was completed, Allāh gave permission to the Prophet to make Hijrah to the ʾAnsār (in al-Madīnah). Some of the Companions has already made Hijrah to al-Habashah before this; and they resided there under the rule of an-Najāshī for some time. The rest of the Companions (in Makkah) made Hijrah to al-Madīnah and when the Prophet settled in al-Madīnah those who migrated to al-Habashah arrived and settled in al-Madīnah, and all praise belongs to Allāh.

The author (رَحِمَهُ ٱللَّهُ) said,

وَالْهِجْرَةُ فَرِيضَةٌ عَلَى هَذِهِ الْأُمَّةِ مِنْ بَلَدِ الشِّرْكِ إِلَى بَلَدِ الْإِسْلَامِ, وَهِيَ بَاقِيَةٌ إِلَى أَنْ تَقُومَ السَّاعَةُ . وَالدَّلِيلُ قَوْلُهُ تَعَالَى: ﴿ إِنَّ ٱلَّذِينَ تَوَفَّىٰهُمُ ٱلْمَلَٰٓئِكَةُ ظَالِمِىٓ أَنفُسِهِمْ قَالُوا۟ فِيمَ كُنتُمْ ۖ قَالُوا۟ كُنَّا مُسْتَضْعَفِينَ فِى ٱلْأَرْضِ ۚ قَالُوٓا۟ أَلَمْ تَكُنْ أَرْضُ ٱللَّهِ وَٰسِعَةً فَتُهَاجِرُوا۟ فِيهَا ۚ فَأُو۟لَٰٓئِكَ مَأْوَىٰهُمْ جَهَنَّمُ ۖ وَسَآءَتْ مَصِيرًا ﴿٩٧﴾ إِلَّا ٱلْمُسْتَضْعَفِينَ مِنَ ٱلرِّجَالِ وَٱلنِّسَآءِ وَٱلْوِلْدَٰنِ لَا يَسْتَطِيعُونَ حِيلَةً وَلَا يَهْتَدُونَ سَبِيلًا ﴿٩٨﴾ فَأُو۟لَٰٓئِكَ عَسَى ٱللَّهُ أَن يَعْفُوَ عَنْهُمْ ۚ وَكَانَ ٱللَّهُ عَفُوًّا غَفُورًا ﴿٩٩﴾ ۞ وَمَن يُهَاجِرْ فِى سَبِيلِ ٱللَّهِ يَجِدْ فِى ٱلْأَرْضِ مُرَٰغَمًا كَثِيرًا وَسَعَةً ۚ وَمَن يَخْرُجْ مِنۢ بَيْتِهِۦ مُهَاجِرًا إِلَى ٱللَّهِ وَرَسُولِهِۦ ثُمَّ يُدْرِكْهُ ٱلْمَوْتُ فَقَدْ وَقَعَ أَجْرُهُۥ عَلَى ٱللَّهِ ۗ وَكَانَ ٱللَّهُ غَفُورًا رَّحِيمًا ﴿١٠٠﴾ ﴾ وَقَوْلُهُ تَعَالَى: ﴿ يَٰعِبَادِىَ ٱلَّذِينَ ءَامَنُوٓا۟ إِنَّ أَرْضِى وَٰسِعَةٌ فَإِيَّٰىَ فَٱعْبُدُونِ ﴿٥٦﴾ ﴾ قَالَ الْبَغَوِيُّ - رَحِمَهُ اللهُ تَعَالَى- : ((سَبَبُ نُزُولِ هَذِهِ الْآيَةِ فِي الْمُسْلِمِينَ الَّذِينَ بِمَكَّةَ : لَمْ يُهَاجِرُوا , نَادَاهُمُ اللهُ بِاسْمِ

الْإِيمَانِ)). وَالدَّلِيلُ عَلَى الْهِجْرَةِ مِنَ السُّنَّةِ قَوْلُهُ (صَلَّى اللهُ عَلَيْهِ وَ سَلَّمَ) : ((لَا تَنْقَطِعُ الْهِجْرَةُ حَتَّى تَنْقَطِعُ التَّوْبَةُ, وَ لَا تَنْقَطِعُ التَّوْبَةُ حَتَّى تَطْلُعَ الشَّمْسُ مِنْ مَغْرِبِهَا)). فَلَمَّا اسْتَقَرَّ فِي الْمَدِينَةِ أُمِرَ بِبَقِيَّةِ شَرَائِعِ الْإِسْلَامِ مِثْلَ الزَّكَاةِ, وَالصَّوْمِ, وَ الْحَجِّ, وَ الْأَذَانِ, وَ الْجِهَادِ, وَ الْأَمْرِ بِالْمَعْرُوفِ, وَ النَّهْيِ عَنِ الْمُنْكَرِ, وَ غَيْرِ ذَلِكَ مِنْ شَرَائِعِ الْإِسْلَامِ. أَخَذَ عَلَى هَذَا عَشْرَ سِنِينَ, ثُمَّ تُوفِيَ -صَلَوَاتُ اللهِ وَ سَلَامُهُ عَلَيْهِ- وَ دِينُهُ بَاقٍ, وَ هَذَا دِينُهُ لَا خَيْرَ إِلَّا دَلَّ الْأُمَّةَ عَلَيْهِ وَ لَا شَرَّ إِلَّا حَذَّرَ مِنْهُ, وَالْخَيْرُ الَّذِي دَلَّ عَلَيْهِ: التَّوْحِيدُ وَ جَمِيعُ مَا يُحِبُّهُ اللهُ وَ يَرْضَاهُ, وَ الشَّرُّ الَّذِي حَذَرَ هَا مِنْهُ: الشِّرْكُ وَ جَمِيعُ مَا يَكْرَهُهُ اللهُ وَ يَأْبَاهُ.

بَعَثَهُ اللهُ إِلَى النَّاسِ كَافَّةً, وَافْتَرَضَ طَاعَتَهُ عَلَى جَمِيعِ الثَّقَلَيْنِ - الْجِنِّ وَ الْإِنْسِ -, وَ الدَّلِيلُ قَوْلُهُ تَعَالَى: ﴿ قُلْ يَٰٓأَيُّهَا ٱلنَّاسُ إِنِّى رَسُولُ ٱللَّهِ إِلَيْكُمْ

جَمِيعًا ﴾ وَ أَكْمَلَ اللهُ بِهِ الدِّينَ, وَ الدَّلِيلُ قَوْلُهُ تَعَالَى
: ﴿ ٱلْيَوْمَ أَكْمَلْتُ لَكُمْ دِينَكُمْ وَأَتْمَمْتُ عَلَيْكُمْ نِعْمَتِي وَرَضِيتُ لَكُمُ ٱلْإِسْلَٰمَ
دِينًا ﴾ وَ الدَّلِيلُ عَلَى مَوْتِهِ (صَلَّى اللهُ عَلَيْهِ وَ سَلَّمَ
) قَوْلُهُ تَعَالَى : ﴿ إِنَّكَ مَيِّتٌ وَإِنَّهُم مَّيِّتُونَ ﴿٣٠﴾ ثُمَّ إِنَّكُمْ يَوْمَ ٱلْقِيَٰمَةِ
عِندَ رَبِّكُمْ تَخْتَصِمُونَ ﴿٣١﴾ ﴾ وَ النَّاسُ إِذَا مَاتُوا يُبْعَثُونَ ,
وَ الدَّلِيلُ قَوْلُهُ تَعَالَى : ﴿ ۞ مِنْهَا خَلَقْنَٰكُمْ وَفِيهَا نُعِيدُكُمْ وَمِنْهَا
نُخْرِجُكُمْ تَارَةً أُخْرَىٰ ﴿٥٥﴾ ﴾ وَ قَوْلُهُ تَعَالَى : ﴿ وَٱللَّهُ أَنۢبَتَكُم مِّنَ
ٱلْأَرْضِ نَبَاتًا ﴿١٧﴾ ثُمَّ يُعِيدُكُمْ فِيهَا وَيُخْرِجُكُمْ إِخْرَاجًا ﴿١٨﴾ ﴾ وَ بَعْدَ
الْبَعْثِ مُحَاسَبُونَ , وَ مَجْزِيُونَ بِأَعْمَالِهِمْ , وَ
الدَّلِيلُ قَوْلُهُ تَعَالَى : ﴿ لِيَجْزِيَ ٱلَّذِينَ أَسَٰٓـُٔواْ بِمَا عَمِلُواْ وَيَجْزِيَ ٱلَّذِينَ
أَحْسَنُواْ بِٱلْحُسْنَى ﴿٣١﴾ ﴾ وَ مَنْ كَذَّبَ بِالْبَعْثِ بَعْدَ الْمَوْتِ
كَفَرَ. وَ الدَّلِيلُ قَوْلُهُ تَعَالَى : ﴿ زَعَمَ ٱلَّذِينَ كَفَرُوٓاْ أَن لَّن يُبْعَثُواْۚ
قُلْ بَلَىٰ وَرَبِّي لَتُبْعَثُنَّ ثُمَّ لَتُنَبَّؤُنَّ بِمَا عَمِلْتُمْۚ وَذَٰلِكَ عَلَى ٱللَّهِ يَسِيرٌ ﴿٧﴾ ﴾

"Hijrah is to move from the lands of Shirk to settle in the land of Islām. This type of immigration is a

religious duty upon this nation and will remain up till the Last Hour.

The evidence is in Allāh's (سُبۡحَانَهُۥوَتَعَالَىٰ) statement,

"Verily! As for those whom the angels take (in death) while they are wronging themselves (as they stayed among the disbelievers even though emigration was obligatory for them), they (angels) say (to them): "In what (condition) were you?" They reply: "We were weak and oppressed on earth." They (angels) say: "Was not the earth of Allah spacious enough for you to emigrate therein?" Such men will find their abode in Hell - What an evil destination! Except the weak ones among men, women and children who cannot devise a plan, nor are they able to direct their way. For these there is hope that Allah will forgive them, and Allah is Ever Oft Pardoning, Oft-Forgiving." [Sūrah an-Nisā' 4:97-99]

And His saying,

"O My slaves who believe! Certainly, spacious is My earth. Therefore, worship Me (Alone)." [Sūrah al-Ankabut 29:56]

Al-Baghawī, (رَحِمَهُ ٱللَّهُ), said, "The reason for revealing this verse to the Muslims in Makkah was that they haven't made Hijrah. Thus, Allāh call out to them in the name of ʾĪmān."

Evidence from the Sunnah is the Prophet's (صَلَّىٰ ٱللَّهُ عَلَيْهِ وَسَلَّمَ) saying,

"Hijrah will not end until repentance ends, and repentance will not end until the sun rises in the west.."

When the Prophet (صَلَّىٰ ٱللَّهُ عَلَيْهِ وَسَلَّمَ) settled in Madīnah, he was ordered with the rest of the legislation. For instances the Zakat, fasting, Pilgrimage, the Adhan (call to prayers), Jihād, commanding the good and forbidding evil, and so on from the legislated matters of Islām.

He remained in Madīnah for ten years after which he (عَلَيْهِ ٱلصَّلَاةُ وَٱلسَّلَامُ) passed away; however his religion remains. This is his religion in which if there was any good he directed his Ummah to it and if there was any evil he warned his Ummah from it. The good in which he directed his Ummah to is Tawhīd and everything Allāh loves and is pleased with. The

evil which he warned his Ummah from is Shirk and everything Allāh detests and rejects.

Allāh has sent him to all people; and He has made it incumbent on all mankind and jinn to obey him. The evidence is in His saying,

"Say (O Muḥammad صَلَّى ٱللَّهُ عَلَيْهِ وَسَلَّمَ): "O mankind! Verily, I am sent to you all as the Messenger of Allāh'" [Sūrah al-ʿArāf 7:158]

With him Allāh has completed and perfected the religion. The evidence is in His saying,

"This day, I have perfected your religion for you, completed My Favour upon you, and have chosen for you Islam as your religion. " [Sūrah al-Māʾidah 5:3]

The evidence of the prophet's death is in His saying,

Verily, you (O Muḥammad صَلَّى ٱللَّهُ عَلَيْهِ وَسَلَّمَ) will die and verily, they (too) will die. Then, on the Day of Resurrection, you will be disputing before your Lord." [Sūrah az-Zumar 39:30-31]

When mankind dies they will be resurrected. The evidence is in His saying,

"Thereof (the earth) We created you, and into it We shall return you, and from it We shall bring you out once again." [Sūrah Tāhā 20:55]

And His saying,

"And Allah has brought you forth from the (dust of) earth. Afterwards He will return you into it (the earth), and bring you forth (again on the Day of Resurrection)?" [Sūrah Nūh 71:17-18]

After Resurrection, they will receive their reckoning before Allāh and they are rewarded or punished. The evidence is in His saying,

"And to Allāh belongs all that is in the heavens and all that is in the earth, that He may requite those who do evil with that which they have done (i.e. punish them in Hell), and reward those who do good, with what is best (i.e. Paradise)." [Sūrah an-Najm 53:31]

Anyone who denies Resurrection is an disbeliever. The evidence is in His saying,

"The disbelievers pretend that they will never be resurrected (for the Account). Say (O Muḥammad صَلَّى ٱللَّهُ عَلَيْهِ وَسَلَّمَ): "Yes! By my Lord, you will certainly be resurrected, then you will be informed of (and recompensed for) what you did, and that is easy for Allāh." [Sūrah at-Taghābun 64:7]

Explanation

When he got settled in Madīnah, he was ordered with the remaining legislations of the Islām, like Zakat, fasting the month of Ramaḍān, and Ḥajj, Jihād, and commanding the good and forbidding the evil. This is because al-Madīnah became the land of Islām, the first capital for Muslims, and that's why they were ordered with these things. Another reason is that they were able to command the good and forbid the evil. **This is a mercy from Allāh (عَزَّوَجَلَّ) that He delayed these obligatory matters until the migration to al-Madīnah.** Originally the Zakat was legislated in Makkah, just as Allāh says in Sūrah Al-ʾAnʿām, which was revealed in Makkah,

﴿ وَءَاتُواْ حَقَّهُۥ يَوۡمَ حَصَادِهِۦۖ ﴾

"on the day of its harvest." [*Sūrah al-ʾAnʿām* 6:141]

However, aspects of Zakat like its portions, it disbursement, details of its rulings didn't occur until the Hijrah to al-Madīnah. The same as for fasting in Ramaḍān was legislated in the second year after the Hijrah.

Hajj was legislated in the ninth or tenth year after the Hijrah. Allāh (سُبۡحَانَهُۥ وَتَعَالَىٰ) revealed, in al-Madīnah, the legislation of Ḥajj in Sūrah ʾĀli ʿImrān,

﴿ وَلِلَّهِ عَلَى ٱلنَّاسِ حِجُّ ٱلۡبَيۡتِ مَنِ ٱسۡتَطَاعَ إِلَيۡهِ سَبِيلٗاۚ ﴾

"And Ḥajj (pilgrimage to Makkah) to the House (Ka'bah) is a duty that mankind owes to Allah, those who can afford the expenses (for one's conveyance, provision and residence)" [*Sūrah ʾĀli ʿImrān* 3:97]

Likewise, Jihād was order in al-Madīnah. Although initially Jihād was only allowed if they were attacked first. Later, they were ordered to initiate fighting. They can attack the disbelievers even if they (disbelievers) didn't start attacking first. So, he would call them to the religion of Allāh and direct them to the right path. So, if they rejected the call (to Tawhīd) they would be fought against them until they accepted Islām. However, the people of the book (the Jews and the Christians)have to pay a Jizyah.

The Majoos (the fire worshippers) were given the same option as the people of the Book. Either they accept Islām or pay the Jizyah (taxes). Yet the rest of the disbelievers it was either Islām or the sword, if the Muslims had the ability to fight against them.

In the tenth year after the Hijrah, the Prophet (صَلَّى ٱللَّهُ عَلَيْهِ وَسَلَّمَ) passed away shortly after Allāh had completed his favor and perfected His religion just Allāh (سُبْحَانَهُ وَتَعَالَىٰ) says,

﴿ ٱلْيَوْمَ أَكْمَلْتُ لَكُمْ دِينَكُمْ وَأَتْمَمْتُ عَلَيْكُمْ نِعْمَتِي وَرَضِيتُ لَكُمُ ٱلْإِسْلَٰمَ دِينًا ﴾

"This day, I have perfected your religion for you, completed My Favor upon you, and have chosen for you Islām as your religion." [*Sūrah al-Māʾidah* 5:3]

He (سُبْحَانَهُ وَتَعَالَىٰ) also says,

﴿ إِنَّكَ مَيِّتٌ وَإِنَّهُم مَّيِّتُونَ ﴿٣٠﴾ ثُمَّ إِنَّكُمْ يَوْمَ ٱلْقِيَٰمَةِ عِندَ رَبِّكُمْ تَخْتَصِمُونَ ﴿٣١﴾ ﴾

"Verily, you (O Muḥammad ﷺ) will die and verily, they (too) will die. Then, on the Day of Resurrection, you will be disputing before your Lord." [Sūrah az-Zumar 39:30-31]

Mankind will be resurrected after they die just as Allāh (سُبْحَانَهُۥ وَتَعَالَىٰ) says,

﴿ وَٱللَّهُ أَنۢبَتَكُم مِّنَ ٱلْأَرْضِ نَبَاتًا ﴿١٧﴾ ثُمَّ يُعِيدُكُمْ فِيهَا وَيُخْرِجُكُمْ إِخْرَاجًا ﴿١٨﴾ ﴾

"And Allāh has brought you forth from the (dust of) earth- Afterwards He will return you into it (the earth), and bring you forth (again on the Day of Resurrection)?" [*Sūrah Nūh* 71:17-18]

He (سُبْحَانَهُۥ وَتَعَالَىٰ) also says,

﴿ زَعَمَ ٱلَّذِينَ كَفَرُوٓاْ أَن لَّن يُبۡعَثُواْۚ قُلۡ بَلَىٰ وَرَبِّي لَتُبۡعَثُنَّ ثُمَّ لَتُنَبَّؤُنَّ بِمَا عَمِلۡتُمۡۚ وَذَٰلِكَ عَلَى ٱللَّهِ يَسِيرٞ ۝٧ ﴾

"The disbelievers thought that they will never be resurrected (for the Account). Say (O Muḥammad ﷺ), Yes! By my Lord, you will certainly be resurrected, then you will be informed of (and recompensed for) what you did, and that is easy for Allāh." [*Sūrah at-Taghābun* 64:7]

He (سُبۡحَانَهُۥ وَتَعَالَىٰ) also says,

﴿ وَلِلَّهِ مَا فِي ٱلسَّمَٰوَٰتِ وَمَا فِي ٱلۡأَرۡضِ لِيَجۡزِيَ ٱلَّذِينَ أَسَٰٓـُٔواْ بِمَا عَمِلُواْ وَيَجۡزِيَ ٱلَّذِينَ أَحۡسَنُواْ بِٱلۡحُسۡنَى ۝٣١ ﴾

"And to Allāh belongs all that is in the heavens and all that is in the earth, that He may punish those who do evil with that which they have done (i.e. punish them in Hell), and reward those who do good, with what is best (i.e. Paradise)." [*Sūrah an-Najm* 53:31]

They will be judged and hold accountable for what they done on the Day of Resurrection. Some of them will be given their books in their right hand while others will receive it in their left hand. So, the happy one will receive his book in his right hand, and the wretched person will receive his book in his left hand.

The happy one's scale (of good deeds) will become heavy. As for the wretched person's scale (of good deeds) will be light and those who commit acts of disobedience are in serious danger. It is possible that their scale can become heavy with repentance, pardoning by Allāh (سُبْحَانَهُ وَتَعَالَىٰ), or good deeds. Likewise, it can be made light and they become of the people of the hell. Thus, they will be punished there for as long as Allāh wills then they will come out because having died upon Islām.

So, it is obligatory for every responsible person to be on guard from sins; they must steadfast upon repentance and righteousness. Because one does not know when his time will come.

One must also have a strong determination, strive against oneself to stay upon the truth, and make sincere repentance for all sins. So, when his end comes and he is upon good and righteousness he will achieve happiness and salvation on the Day of Resurrection.

EXPLANATION OF WHAT ALLĀH HAS SENT THE MESSENGER WITH:

The author (رَحِمَهُ ٱللَّهُ) said,

﴿وَ أَرْسَلُ جَمِيعَ الرُّسُلِ مُبَشِّرِينَ وَ مُنْذِرِينَ , وَ الدَّلِيلُ قَوْلُهُ تَعَالَى: ﴿رُّسُلًا مُّبَشِّرِينَ وَمُنذِرِينَ لِئَلَّا يَكُونَ لِلنَّاسِ عَلَى ٱللَّهِ حُجَّةٌۢ بَعْدَ ٱلرُّسُلِ﴾ وَ أَوَّلُهُمْ نُوحٌ (عَلَيْهِ السَّلَام) , وَ آخِرُهُمْ مُحَمَّدٌ (صَلَّى اللهُ عَلَيْهِ وَ سَلَّمَ) مُحَمَّدٌ (صَلَّى اللهُ عَلَيْهِ وَ سَلَّمَ) خَاتَمُ النَّبِيِّينَ. وَ الدَّلِيلُ عَلَى أَنَّ أَوَّلَهُمْ نُوحٌ قَوْلُهُ تَعَالَى: ﴿إِنَّآ أَوْحَيْنَآ إِلَيْكَ كَمَآ أَوْحَيْنَآ إِلَىٰ نُوحٍ وَٱلنَّبِيِّـۧنَ مِنۢ بَعْدِهِۦ﴾. وَ كُلُّ أُمَّةٍ بَعَثَ اللهُ إِلَيْهَا رَسُولاً مِنْ نُوحٍ

إِلَى مُحَمَّدٍ (صَلَّى اللهُ عَلَيْهِ وَ سَلَّمَ) يَأْمُرُهُمْ بِعِبَادَةِ اللهِ وَحْدَهُ, وَ يَنْهَاهُمْ عَنْ عِبَادَةِ الطَّاغُوتِ. وَ الدَّلِيلُ قَوْلُهُ تَعَالَى: ﴿ وَلَقَدْ بَعَثْنَا فِي كُلِّ أُمَّةٍ رَّسُولًا أَنِ ٱعْبُدُوا۟ ٱللَّهَ وَٱجْتَنِبُوا۟ ٱلطَّٰغُوتَ ﴾ وَ افْتَرَضَ اللهُ عَلَى جَمِيعِ الْعِبَادِ الْكُفْرَ بِالطَّاغُوتِ, وَالإِيْمَانُ بِاللهِ. قَالَ ابْنُ الْقَيِّمِ - رَحِمَهُ اللهُ تَعَالَى - : (مَعْنَى (الطَّاغُوتِ) : مَا تَجَاوَزَ بِهِ الْعَبْدُ حَدَّهُ مِنْ مَعْبُودٍ أَوْ مَتْبُوعٍ أَوْ مُطَاعٍ)). وَ الطَّوَاغِيتُ كَثِيرَةٌ رُؤُوسُهُمْ خَمْسَةٌ: إِبْلِيسُ لَعَنَهُ اللهُ, وَمَنْ عُبِدَ وَهُوَ رَاضٍ وَمَنْ دَعَا النَّاسَ إِلَى عِبَادَةِ نَفْسِهِ وَمَنْ دُعِيَ شَيْئًا مِنْ عِلْمِ الْغَيْبِ وَ مَنْ حَكَمَ بِغَيْرِ مَا أَنْزَلَ اللهُ, وَالدَّلِيلُ قَوْلُهُ تَعَالَى: ﴿ لَآ إِكْرَاهَ فِى ٱلدِّينِ ۖ قَد تَّبَيَّنَ ٱلرُّشْدُ مِنَ ٱلْغَىِّ ۚ فَمَن يَكْفُرْ بِٱلطَّٰغُوتِ وَيُؤْمِنۢ بِٱللَّهِ فَقَدِ ٱسْتَمْسَكَ بِٱلْعُرْوَةِ ٱلْوُثْقَىٰ لَا ٱنفِصَامَ لَهَا ۗ وَٱللَّهُ سَمِيعٌ عَلِيمٌ ﴿٢٥٦﴾ ﴾ وَهَذَا مَعْنَى لَا إِلَهَ إِلَّا اللهُ. وَ فِي الْحَدِيثِ: ((رَأْسُ الْأَمْرِ الْإِسْلَامِ, وَعَمُودُهُ الصَّلَاةُ, وَ ذِرْوَةُ سَنَامِهِ الْجِهَادُ فِي

سَبِيلِ اللهِ))، وَ اللهُ أَعْلَمُ. وَ صَلَّى اللهُ عَلَى نَبِيِّنَا مُحَمَّدٍ، وَ عَلَى آلِهِ وَ صَحْبِهِ وَ سَلَّمَ.

"Allāh has sent all the messengers as bearers of glad tidings and warners. The evidence is in His (سُبْحَانَهُ وَتَعَالَىٰ) saying:

"Messengers as bearers of good news as well as of warning in order that mankind should have no plea against Allāh after the Messengers." [Sūrah an-Nisā᾽ 4:165]

The first messenger was Nūh (عَلَيْهِ ٱلصَّلَاةُ وَٱلسَّلَامُ) and the last was Muḥammad (صَلَّى ٱللَّهُ عَلَيْهِ وَسَلَّمَ). who he is the Seal (Last) of the prophets. The evidence that the first messenger is Nūh is in His saying,

"Verily, We have inspired you (O Muḥammad صَلَّى ٱللَّهُ عَلَيْهِ وَسَلَّمَ) as We inspired Nūh (Noah) and the Prophets after him." [Sūrah an-Nisā᾽ 4:163]

Every nation, from the time of Nūh to Muḥammad (صَلَّى ٱللَّهُ عَلَيْهِ وَسَلَّمَ), was sent a Messenger to order them to

worship Allāh alone, and to forbid them from worshiping idols. The evidence is in His saying:

"And verily, We have sent among every Ummah (community, nation) a Messenger (proclaiming): "Worship Allāh (Alone), and avoid (or keep away from) Tāghūt (all false deities, etc. i.e. do not worship Tāghūt besides Allāh).'" [Sūrah an-Nahl 16:36]

Allāh has made it religiously incumbent upon all mankind to disbelieve in Tāghūt and to believe in Him.

Ibn Al-Qayyim (رَحِمَهُ ٱللَّٰهُ) said, "at-Tāghūt refers to the limits that the servant exceeds, as regards to a deity, one whom is followed, or given . obedience."

The Tawaghīt (false deities) are many, but the main ones are five:

1. **Shayṭān, may Allāh curse him,**
2. **Whosoever is worshipped and is acquiesce to that worship,**
3. **Whosoever calls people to worship him,**

4. **Whosoever claims to have any knowledge of the Unseen (Ghayb), and**

5. **Whosoever judges or rules according to whatever has not been sent down by Allāh.**

The evidence is in His saying,

"There is no compulsion in religion. Verily, the Right Path has become distinct from the wrong path. Whoever disbelieves in Taghut and believes in Allah, then he has grasped the most trustworthy handhold that will never break. And Allah is All-Hearer, All-Knower." [Sūrah al-Baqarah 2:256]

This is the meaning of "La ilaha illa Allāh" (There is no deity worthy of worship, in truth, except Allāh)."

In the Ḥadīth, "The head of the matter is Islām, its pillar is the prayer and its peak is Jihād."

And Allāh knows best.

Explanation

The Messenger (صَلَّى ٱللَّهُ عَلَيْهِ وَسَلَّمَ) was sent to all of mankind, Jinn and mankind, just as Allāh (سُبْحَانَهُ وَتَعَالَىٰ) says,

﴿ قُلْ يَـٰٓأَيُّهَا ٱلنَّاسُ إِنِّى رَسُولُ ٱللَّهِ إِلَيْكُمْ جَمِيعًا ﴾

"Say (O Muḥammad صَلَّى ٱللَّهُ عَلَيْهِ وَسَلَّمَ): "O mankind! Verily, I am sent to you all as the Messenger of Allāh." [*Sūrah al-'Arāf* 7:158]

He (سُبْحَانَهُ وَتَعَالَىٰ) also says,

﴿ وَمَآ أَرْسَلْنَـٰكَ إِلَّا كَآفَّةً لِّلنَّاسِ بَشِيرًا وَنَذِيرًا ﴾

"And We have not sent you (O Muḥammad صَلَّى ٱللَّهُ عَلَيْهِ وَسَلَّمَ) except as a giver of glad tidings and a warner to all mankind, but most of men know not." [*Sūrah Saba* 34:28]

He is the seal of the prophets who no prophet will come after him.

Likewise, all of the messengers were sent to their respected nations as warners and givers of glad tidings. From the first of them to the last of them. Nūh was the first of the

﴿ رُّسُلًا مُّبَشِّرِينَ وَمُنذِرِينَ لِئَلَّا يَكُونَ لِلنَّاسِ عَلَى ٱللَّهِ حُجَّةُۢ بَعْدَ ٱلرُّسُلِۚ ﴾

"Messengers as bearers of good news as well as of warning in order that mankind should have no plea against Allāh after the Messengers." [*Sūrah an-Nisā'* 4:165]

Allāh's statement, **"Bearer of good"** refers to the Messengers gave glad tidings of Paradise to those who were obedient to them. Allāh's statement, **"warning"** are those who warned the people from committing acts of Shirk, the Hell fire, and the painful torment if they disobey Allāh.

In the same fashion Muḥammad (ﷺ) was sent as a bearer of good and a warner just as Allāh (سُبْحَانَهُ وَتَعَالَىٰ) says,

﴿ يَٰٓأَيُّهَا ٱلنَّبِيُّ إِنَّآ أَرْسَلْنَٰكَ شَٰهِدًا وَمُبَشِّرًا وَنَذِيرًا ۝٤٥ وَدَاعِيًا إِلَى ٱللَّهِ بِإِذْنِهِۦ وَسِرَاجًا مُّنِيرًا ۝٤٦ ﴾

"O Prophet (Muḥammad ﷺ)! Verily, We have sent you as witness, and a bearer of glad tidings, and

a warner, -- And as one who invites to Allāh [Islāmic Monotheism, i.e. to worship none but Allāh (Alone)] by His Leave, and as a lamp spreading light (through your instructions from the Qur'ān and the Sunnah the legal ways of the Prophet صَلَّى ٱللَّهُ عَلَيْهِ وَسَلَّمَ).” [*Sūrah al-Ahzāb* 33:45-46]

He (سُبْحَانَهُ وَتَعَالَىٰ) also says,

﴿ مَّا كَانَ مُحَمَّدٌ أَبَآ أَحَدٍ مِّن رِّجَالِكُمْ وَلَٰكِن رَّسُولَ ٱللَّهِ وَخَاتَمَ ٱلنَّبِيِّـۧنَ ﴾

“Muḥammad (صَلَّى ٱللَّهُ عَلَيْهِ وَسَلَّمَ) is not the father of any man among you, but he is the Messenger of Allāh and the last (end) of the Prophets.” [*Sūrah al-Ahzāb* 33:40]

So, it is mandatory upon all nations to follow their messenger. Following their and submitting to what their Messengers came with of guidance was a religious duty upon every nation. Allāh had promised every nation happiness in this world and the hereafter, yet many of them disobeyed their messengers and went against what they came with. Allāh says,

﴿ وَمَآ أَكۡثَرُ ٱلنَّاسِ وَلَوۡ حَرَصۡتَ بِمُؤۡمِنِينَ ١٠٣ ﴾

"And most of mankind will not believe even if you desire it eagerly." [*Sūrah Yūsuf* 12:103]

He (سُبۡحَانَهُۥوَتَعَالَىٰ) also says,

﴿ وَإِن تُطِعۡ أَكۡثَرَ مَن فِي ٱلۡأَرۡضِ يُضِلُّوكَ عَن سَبِيلِ ٱللَّهِۚ ﴾

"And if you obey most of those on earth, they will mislead you far away from Allāh's Path. They follow nothing but conjectures, and they do nothing but lie." [Sūrah al-ʾAnʿām 6:116]

He (سُبۡحَانَهُۥوَتَعَالَىٰ) also says,

﴿ وَقَلِيلٌ مِّنۡ عِبَادِيَ ٱلشَّكُورُ ١٣ ﴾

"But few of My slaves are grateful." [*Sūrah Saba* 34:13]

He (سُبۡحَانَهُۥوَتَعَالَىٰ) also says,

﴿ وَلَقَدْ صَدَّقَ عَلَيْهِمْ إِبْلِيسُ ظَنَّهُۥ فَٱتَّبَعُوهُ إِلَّا فَرِيقًا مِّنَ ٱلْمُؤْمِنِينَ ٢٠ ﴾

"And indeed Iblis (Shayṭān) did prove true his thought about them, and they followed him, all except a group of true believers (in the Oneness of Allāh)." [*Sūrah as-Saba'* 34:20]

Every messenger called their nation to the Tawhīd of Allāh, obedience to Him, and the abandonment of Shirk and acts of disobedience. Allāh (سُبْحَانَهُ وَتَعَالَىٰ) says,

﴿ وَلَقَدْ بَعَثْنَا فِى كُلِّ أُمَّةٍ رَّسُولًا أَنِ ٱعْبُدُوا۟ ٱللَّهَ وَٱجْتَنِبُوا۟ ٱلطَّٰغُوتَ ﴾

"And verily, We have sent among every Ummah (community, nation) a Messenger (proclaiming): "Worship Allāh (Alone), and avoid (or keep away from) Tāghūt (all false deities, etc. i.e. do not worship Tāghūt besides Allāh)." [Sūrah an-Nahl 16:36]

Allah's statement, "Worship Allāh" refers to obeying Him, worshipping Him alone, being upright upon his religion, and staying away from worshiping Tāghūt (false deities).

The word at-Tāghūt is everything that is worshipped besides Allāh and he is satisfied with it, anyone that rules with other than what Allāh sent or who calls to it. The word Tāghūt is taken from the word Tūghyān which means to go beyond limits.

So, Tāghūt is a person that exceeds the limit either by committing Shirk, an act of disbelief, or calling to that. The most evil of them and the leader of them is Iblis, may Allāh curse n him.

In the same fashion, whoever that calls to the worship of himself, or is pleased with being worshiped beside Allāh like Fir'awn and Nimrod, or whoever claims to have knowledge of the unseen like magicians, psychics, and wizards.

Likewise, whoever rules with other than what Allāh ordered on deliberately. All of these individuals are Tawaghīt (plural for Tāghūt) all of who have exceeded limits (concerning worship), and have disobeyed Allāh.

Allāh (سُبْحَانَهُ وَتَعَالَىٰ) says,

﴿ لَآ إِكْرَاهَ فِى ٱلدِّينِ ۖ قَد تَّبَيَّنَ ٱلرُّشْدُ مِنَ ٱلْغَىِّ ۚ ﴾

"There is no compulsion in religion. Verily, the Right Path has become distinct from the wrong path)." [*Sūrah al-Baqarah* 2:256]

The **"Right Path (Rushd)"** refers to the religion of Islām and what the Prophet (صَلَّى ٱللَّهُ عَلَيْهِ وَسَلَّمَ) came with; and **"the wrong path (Ghayy)"** refers to the disbelief in Allāh and misguidance.

He (سُبْحَانَهُ وَتَعَالَىٰ)says,

﴿ فَمَن يَكْفُرْ بِٱلطَّٰغُوتِ وَيُؤْمِنۢ بِٱللَّهِ فَقَدِ ٱسْتَمْسَكَ بِٱلْعُرْوَةِ ٱلْوُثْقَىٰ لَا ٱنفِصَامَ لَهَا ۗ وَٱللَّهُ سَمِيعٌ عَلِيمٌ ﴿٢٥٦﴾ ﴾

"Whoever disbelieves in Tāghūt and believes in Allāh, then he has grasped the most trustworthy handhold that will never break. And Allāh is All-Hearer, All-Knower." [*Sūrah al-Baqarah* 2:256]

Allāh's statement, **"disbelieves in Tāghūt"** refers to disavowing oneself from the Tāghūt (false deity), believing it is false, and consequently disavowing oneself from Shirk.

The statement, **"believes in Allāh"** refers to believing that Allāh is the only one to be worshipped, that He is true deity, that he believes in the legislation and Muḥammad (عَلَيْهِ ٱلصَّلَاةُ وَٱلسَّلَامُ) and submits to all of that. This is the (real) believer.

Then Allāh says, **"then he has grasped"** meaning he has gripped to **"the most trustworthy handhold"** which is the statement 'La ilaha ila Allāh' the statement of Tawhīd (pure monotheism) meaning he has gripped on a handhold that will never break. Rather, whoever grasps to it with sincerity and is upright upon that will enter paradise. Because the statement of Tawhīd has rights which are singling out Allāh alone in worship, obeying Him, and adhering to His legislation.

Muḥammad is the seal of the prophets and messengers. He was sent as a messenger to all the people of earth, from jinn and mankind. Thus, it is obligatory upon every Muslim who is held accountable to obey him, follow his legislation, and not oppose it (legislation). All of the previous legislations have been abrogated by the coming of his legislation (عَلَيْهِ ٱلصَّلَاةُ وَٱلسَّلَامُ) just like Allāh (سُبْحَانَهُ وَتَعَالَىٰ) says,

﴿ يَـٰٓأَيُّهَا ٱلنَّاسُ إِنِّى رَسُولُ ٱللَّهِ إِلَيْكُمْ جَمِيعًا ﴾

"Say (O Muḥammad صَلَّى ٱللَّهُ عَلَيْهِ وَسَلَّمَ): "O mankind! Verily, I am sent to you all as the Messenger of Allāh." [*Sūrah al-ʿArāf* 7:158]

Just before that Allāh says,

﴿ فَٱلَّذِينَ ءَامَنُوا۟ بِهِۦ وَعَزَّرُوهُ وَنَصَرُوهُ وَٱتَّبَعُوا۟ ٱلنُّورَ ٱلَّذِىٓ أُنزِلَ مَعَهُۥٓ ۙ أُو۟لَـٰٓئِكَ هُمُ ٱلْمُفْلِحُونَ ﴿١٥٧﴾ ﴾

"So those who believe in him (Muḥammad صَلَّى ٱللَّهُ عَلَيْهِ وَسَلَّمَ), honor him, help him, and follow the light (the Qur'ān) which has been sent down with him, it is they who will be successful." [*Sūrah al-ʿArāf* 7:157]

He (سُبْحَانَهُ وَتَعَالَىٰ) also says,

﴿ وَمَن يَكْفُرْ بِهِۦ مِنَ ٱلْأَحْزَابِ فَٱلنَّارُ مَوْعِدُهُۥ ۚ ﴾

"but those of the sects (Jews, Christians and all the other non-Muslim nations) that reject it (the Qur'ān), the Fire will be their promised meeting-place." [*Sūrah Hūd* 11:17]

and the Prophet (ﷺ) said,

وَالَّذِي نَفْسُ مُحَمَّدٍ بِيَدِهِ لاَ يَسْمَعُ بِي أَحَدٌ مِنْ هَذِهِ الأُمَّةِ يَهُودِيٌّ وَلاَ نَصْرَانِيٌّ ثُمَّ يَمُوتُ وَلَمْ يُؤْمِنْ بِالَّذِي أُرْسِلْتُ بِهِ إِلاَّ كَانَ مِنْ أَصْحَابِ النَّارِ

"By Him in Whose hand is the life of Muḥammad, he who amongst the community of Jews or Christians hears about me, but does not affirm his belief in that with which I have been sent and dies in this state (of disbelief), he shall be but one of the companions of the Hell-Fire)."[12]

The verses and aḥādith concerning this matter are numerous. The people of knowledge (رَحِمَهُمُ ٱللَّهُ) have agreed that it is not allowed for anyone from this 'Ummah to be in outright opposition to the legislation of Muḥammad

[12] Ṣaḥīḥ Muslim No. (153) from the Ḥadīth of Abū Hurayrah (رَضِيَ ٱللَّهُ عَنْهُ).

(صَلَّى ٱللَّهُ عَلَيْهِ وَسَلَّمَ). So, whoever believes in that has committed an act of disbelief which takes him out of the fold of Islām. We ask Allāh for wellbeing and safety from that.

In the Ḥadīth,

رَأْسُ الْأَمْرِ الْإِسْلَامُ ، وَ عَمُودُهُ الصَّلَاةُ ، وَ ذِرْوَةُ سَنَامِهِ الْجِهادُ فِي سَبِيلِ اللهِ

"The head of the matter is Islām, and its pillar is the Ṣalāh, and its peak is Jihad for the sake of Allāh."

It is a religiously binding upon every duty bound Muslim to single out Allāh alone in worship, disbelieve and reject the worship of every Tāghūt (false deity), strictly adhere to Tawhīd, follow Allāh's legislation, and give great importance His commands and prohibitions.

The Prophet's (صَلَّى ٱللَّهُ عَلَيْهِ وَسَلَّمَ) statement, **"The head of the matter"** refers to the head of the religion which is Islām. Islām is to make the testimony that none has the right to be worshiped in truth except Allāh and that Muḥammad is the messenger of Allāh. So, whoever is duty bound to that testimony enters the religion of Islām.

"and its pillar is the Ṣalāh" is the second and greatest pillar after the two testimonies of faith. Then follows Zakat, fasting, Hajj, and the rest of Allāh's orders.

"and its peak is Jihad for the sake of Allāh" because by this the religion is preserved, safeguarded, people are called to the true religion of Allāh, and the people remain steadfast upon the truth. Thus, this is the peak of the religion from the aspect of what it contains preserving the religion, calling to the truth, and Allāh knows best.